FRANZ SCHUBERT
AND THE ESSENCE OF MELODY

Hans Gal

FRANZ SCHUBERT
AND THE ESSENCE
OF MELODY

———

LONDON
VICTOR GOLLANCZ LTD
1974

ISBN 0 575 01559 4

I am greatly indebted to my wife Hanna and to my daughter and son-in-law, Eva and Tony Fox, for their generous assistance in the preparation of the English edition of this book.

H. G.

Printed in Great Britain by
The Camelot Press Ltd, London and Southampton

To my wife
Hanna

CONTENTS

PREFACE

SINCE THE APPEARANCE of Otto Erich Deutsch's documentary biography, containing all the available contemporary sources, there is hardly any uncertainty concerning the essential facts of Schubert's life. His music was published in a Complete Edition (1888–97), to which nothing of major importance has had to be added since, and the chronology of his works, with rare exceptions, has been exactly established. The end and aim of the present book is therefore not research into biographical or bibliographical detail, but a closer approach to the secrets of Schubert's art and character, the background of his creative individuality, and the peculiarities of his style, which have so often been misjudged and misinterpreted. Anyone who has the gift of spontaneous artistic appreciation will feel that the solution to all riddles, the answer to all questions, is to be found in the music itself. It might be doubted whether there is any point in attempting to approach by way of the intellect things that should be felt directly and intuitively. If I nevertheless set out to do this, it is due to the experience that all too often access is blocked by prejudice and impressions are obstructed by a lack of readiness to submit to them. Both musicians and music-lovers are extraordinarily susceptible to suggestions derived from reading or hearsay, quite apart from being almost inevitably subject to misconceptions with which they have grown up. In view of this, it may be justifiable to attempt by means of analysis to penetrate to the core of the matter, the music itself, and thus to arrive at a direct appreciation of the essence of an art which reaches to such depths of human feeling as does that of Schubert.

As politicians have long known, the saying "lies are short-lived" is unduly optimistic. Lies have a long life, and misunderstandings live still longer. The judgment of posterity will probably be just in the end, but it takes a desperately long time to be reached, and this rarely happens without appeal or plea of nullity.

INTRODUCTION

Mich umwohnet mit glänzendem Aug' das Volk der Phaiaken;
Immer ist's Sonntag, es dreht immer am Herd sich der Spiess.
SCHILLER

(In the midst of the tribe of the bright-eyed Phaeacians I dwell;
Eternally Sunday, and aye turns the spit by the fire.)

NO MUSIC IS loved as much as Schubert's. Of all the great
composers it is he whose tunes have attained the widest popularity, because they so directly seize the imagination. And none
of the great has had to pay so high a price for his fame. He
became an operetta hero, his melodies commercial products.
And even now the general image of him is still like a genre
painting: he is seen attired in the *Biedermeier* style of his period,
with a good-natured smile, the ideal representative of Viennese
ease and cosiness, of the philistine pleasures of long-departed
good old days, a lowly schoolmaster and a humble fiddler.

This image was not created by the operettas and ballets in
which his person and his music appeared. It was there right
from the start and was what made these Schubert ballets,
Schubert operettas and Schubert novels possible in the first
place. This is how he was seen by his friends and contemporaries,
this is how they described him. It often happens that a great
man lives in a kind of incognito: consciously or unconsciously
he chooses his mask, and it takes a considerable time for the
real face to appear from behind the mask. Just as "papa Haydn"
proved a convenient label which permitted the philistine to
approach a genius without ceremony and to pat him on the
shoulder, so *Schwammerl*, "little mushroom", the nickname
Schubert's friends had given him because of his small, plump
appearance, became his picture for the world. The true stature
of Haydn seems to have been recognised only during the last
few decades as the gigantic scope of his work has become more
and more apparent. With regard to Schubert, the world still
does not seem to have progressed beyond the *Schwammerl* image.

He himself certainly never contradicted this notion. He needed it as a shield against trivial curiosity, as a protection for the artist's most essential, most secret possession, the tabernacle of his creative soul, which, shunning the light, is sensitive to touch like a mimosa. Instinctively the artist seeks the mask which will best enable him to come to a tolerable arrangement with the world and its everyday demands. The mask he chooses will depend on his character. What he needs is a minimum of living space, a secure domain behind invisible walls where he can live unmolested with his dreams, his visions. His most essential requirement is to be undisturbed, the very thing which the world, with its inescapable bustle, its urge to enter a realm that seems so strange and wonderful and to which such an elect has the key, is least ready to grant him. Against such intrusion one artist will cover himself with prickly armour, another will pad himself with everyday banality. Schubert chatted, strolled, laughed and drank with his friends. For them he was *Schwammerl*, their trusty companion in innocent amusements, one of them, a pleasure-loving philistine. And he evidently needed this element of relief in his life; he was so young, so full of the joy of living, so much in need of relaxation. Lacking any ambition as to his position in the world, devoted entirely and with the fullest intensity to his creative work, he found that the most convenient attitude to adopt was that which demanded the least extra effort. His life was cut off in its prime; his work, colossal as it is, remained a torso. Even Mozart, who died so young, was anchored very much more deeply in the consciousness of his contemporaries when he passed away at thirty-six than was the thirty-one-year-old Schubert, who, outside a narrow circle of friends, as yet hardly existed for the world. Franz Grillparzer, the poet, who belonged to the periphery of this circle and wrote poems for Schubert, shows unconsciously in the epitaph he composed for him how the world regarded him at that time:

> Death has buried here rich treasure,
> but still fairer hopes.

This, in the reverent parlance of a necrologue, hardly means more than "a gifted young man—what a pity he had to go!"

That this was roughly in accordance with the general view is clearly borne out by the fact that, with the exception of a number of songs published soon after his death, nobody in Vienna showed even the slightest interest in this "rich treasure", let alone raised a finger to dig it up. The first person to initiate anything of this kind was Robert Schumann, who visited Vienna ten years after Schubert's death and, at his brother Ferdinand's, found huge piles of manuscripts which until then no one had even deemed worth looking at. It was thanks to the immediate steps he took that the Great C major Symphony had its first performance in Leipzig, under Mendelssohn's baton, and that a list of the available manuscripts was published, after which, not without hesitation, some publishers became interested. But how far away the world then was from even sensing the greatness of Schubert's work!

An outstanding achievement can be misunderstood for various reasons. Bach was wrongly assessed because he appeared too "learned", Schubert because he seemed to lack such learning. The one could not be forgiven for making access to his music so difficult, the other for making it so easy. Should anyone find this statement bizarre, I would refer him to the first comprehensive Schubert biography by Heinrich Kreissle (1865) who, though an enthusiastic Schubertian, can dismiss a work of such eternally fresh beauty as the "Trout" Quintet with the words "melodious and tame", and can call a supreme achievement like the Octet "a not particularly deep, but charming and stimulating work". When in 1853 one of Schubert's most magnificent works, the String Quintet in C major, was published, Joseph Joachim, otherwise an impassioned apostle of Schubert's chamber music, could not suppress some critical reservations about its "shapelessness". If sincere admirers could make such judgments at that time, one must not be surprised if a less amicably disposed critic, Richard Wagner, simply failed to understand what on earth his friend Liszt could see in Schubert's "philistine sonatas and trios". The healthy instinct of music lovers, however, proved more reliable; every one of Schubert's works that came before the public found an appreciative audience.

Liszt had already contributed to this public interest, only a few years after Schubert's death, with brilliant paraphrases of his songs and dance tunes, though of course he arranged them in his own particular way and as a virtuoso pianist. He called such pieces *Hommage aux Dames de Vienne* or *Soirées de Vienne*, and he was the first, though undoubtedly with the best intentions, to turn Schubert's music into light entertainment, as was done later in a much cruder way.

It is hardly necessary to point out that successes of this kind are not without danger for the reputation of a composer whose image is as yet scarcely defined with the public. Major works had to wait for decades. The Octet, the String Quartet in G major, and the above-mentioned String Quintet were kept in the vaults of a Vienna publisher and did not appear until after the middle of the century, while the B minor Symphony and Schubert's greatest choral work, the Mass in E flat, did not appear until 1865. And two years later George Grove, the English musicologist, was still able to discover in Vienna, amongst other unprinted works, the manuscript of Schubert's music to *Rosamunde*, which he could subsequently make available to the world. In fact, "discover" is not the right term: the existence of the manuscript, owned by Schubert's nephew Eduard Schneider, was known, and Kreissle had mentioned it in his biography. But nobody had taken any interest.

The large Complete Edition of Schubert's works, which appeared thirty years later, containing an abundance of hitherto unpublished music, offered for the first time a full survey of a life's work of inconceivable richness. But, for all that, the conflict of opinions was still far from settled. Against the ever-growing popularity of Schubert's music can be set the utterances of such serious scholars and musicians as Romain Rolland, Sir Hubert Parry, or Vincent d'Indy, who felt compelled to expostulate against his inadequate writing-technique, lack of self-criticism, and faulty form-construction. This is harmless compared with a feat of George Bernard Shaw, who, before becoming famous as a playwright, was a respected music critic in London. It gives one food for thought that an artist of his stature was able, forty years later, and at the peak of his international fame, to have a review like the following, on Schubert's Great C major Symphony, reprinted, instead of being ashamed of having written it, and glad that it had been forgotten:

In the Crystal Palace there is an understanding among the regular frequenters that a performance of Schubert's Symphony in C is one of the specialities of the place. The analytic programme of it is one of Sir George Grove's masterpieces—and Mr. Manns [the conductor] always receives a special ovation at the end. The band rises to the occasion with its greatest splendour; and I have to make a point of looking pleased, lest Sir George should turn my way and, reading my inmost thoughts, cut me dead for ever afterwards. For it seems to me all but wicked to give the public so irresistible a description of all the manifold charms and winningness of this astonishing symphony and not tell him, on the other side of the question, the lamentable truth that a more exasperatingly brainless composition was never put on paper.

One year later, in 1893, G.B.S. writes of a symphony by Hermann Goetz, an amiable and all-but-forgotten German composer of the seventies: "Beside it, Schubert's symphonies seem mere debauches of exquisite musical thoughtlessness. Goetz has the charm of Schubert without his brainlessness."

It is no consolation that in the three volumes of George Bernard Shaw's collected music reviews, published in 1932, equally absurd attacks on Brahms or Verdi can be found. But when a celebrated author writes such things, one must not be surprised if less famous ones repeat them, particularly as there is no greater satisfaction for a small mind than to find fault with a great one. Not many years ago one of the leading English music magazines published an article with the title "Tales from the Vienna Backwoods", in which Schubert is sentenced to death and executed without ceremony.[1] This would hardly be worth mentioning, except that it is remarkable that a periodical of international standing should have printed such a thing. Here one can read: "I have never heard a convincing reason why we should accept, as a great genius, a composer so representative of the curiously trivial phase of culture in which he lived; nor why, even admitting the quality of the few works in which he surpassed himself, we should be obliged to admire his commonplace average as though it were an inspired revelation." Or, on the Symphony in C major: "No wonder the Phil-

[1] See *Music and Letters*, London, 1962, p. 38.

harmonic Orchestra in London laughed at it in 1844. And when it comes to the songs, what is there about them to justify their reputation? 'Das Wandern' is the incarnation of common-place; 'Who is Sylvia?' might be addressed to a *Bierkeller* barmaid but not to a heroine of Shakespeare; 'Heidenröslein' and 'Die Post' are as cheap as their words (is it possible to endure the words 'mein Herz' again after the hearing of the latter?); 'The Trout' (as also the variations on it in the Quintet) seems to me to typify the greater part of Schubert's output in the quality of meeting-ground for spiritual obtuseness and poverty of musical invention. . . . An unsubtle mentality, then, expressed through a medium of an all but exhausted idiom; and taking an unconscionable time over the expression. . . ."

These are excesses of animosity. Yet they characterise a situation in which delight in Schubert's music is confronted with an obstinate refusal to take him seriously. To what extent the questionable component of Schubert's popularity, his exploitation by the entertainment industry, has contributed to this, cannot even be approximately assessed. One thing, however, must be said: one cannot dismiss certain objections which are repeated again and again simply by denying their foundation. For once the whole problem has to be faced impartially, namely the fact that serious aesthetic questions are posed in Schubert's music, and that, even in the realm of the highest artistic achievements, contradictions may arise between generally accepted principles and individual solutions, contradictions which have to be cleared up in order to prevent reason from turning into nonsense and knowledge into blindness.

As an ironical sequel to Schubert's destiny as a humble suppliant, a trivial occurrence may be mentioned. In the archives of the Vienna Philharmonic Orchestra there is preserved a letter written in 1895 by Schubert's youngest brother Andreas (born 1823) and addressed to the administration of this famous orchestra. In it he asks for admittance to a forthcoming performance of his brother's Great C major Symphony.

This request was turned down with polite regret.

A HUMBLE LIFE

IN AUSTRIA, THE schoolmaster's profession has always been respectable, and always poorly paid. Franz Schubert, the father, had moved from Moravia to Vienna, where at first he became an assistant teacher in a school run by a brother of his. In 1785 he took over a school in Lichtenthal, a suburb of Vienna, and married Elizabeth Vietz, a servant girl who hailed from Silesia. It was a hard-working lower middle-class family. Of fourteen children only five survived. The fourth of them was Franz Peter, born on 31 January 1797. The house of his birth in the Nussdorferstrasse, in the ninth district of Vienna, is still intact. It now contains a Schubert museum.

The love of music, and a talent for it, is an Austrian heritage. Besides other qualifications, a schoolmaster in Vienna was expected to have some knowledge of music. Father Schubert liked to have music at home, and the boy, whose talent manifested itself at an early stage without any fuss being made about it, was soon able to join in at the piano or with the violin. After his father had taught him the rudiments, Michael Holzer, choir-master at the Lichtenthal parish church, became his first teacher. He took the boy into his choir, and as he showed intelligence and had a nice voice, the obvious course was to try to have him admitted to the Court Chapel, which offered all sorts of advantages and where there was always demand for gifted choir-boys. After he had successfully passed the entrance examination, the eleven-year-old Franz Schubert was granted a place there under the Court conductors Salieri and Eybler. Seventy years earlier, Joseph Haydn had had a similar training at St Stephen's in Vienna. The general schooling Schubert received at the Court Chapel was better than that which Haydn had been given, since the Court Chapel had its own residential school providing the usual secondary education of the time. Considering the circumstances of the period, one can assume that such an education was still rather limited. The "good" Emperor Francis—he probably assumed this attribute himself, as his subjects had little cause to call him so—once said to a deputation of schoolmasters: "I don't need scholars. I need obedient subjects." He had steered his empire tolerably through the tossings of the Napoleonic wars, through defeats and state bankruptcy. As far as the submissiveness of his subjects was concerned, he would stand for no nonsense. But he was the last reigning Hapsburg who still preserved the active interest in music that had been traditional in his family for centuries, and he was sufficiently musical to confine himself to the second fiddle when playing string quartets, one of his chief hobbies.

The patriarchal despotism of his era was mirrored in family life by unconditional paternal authority. And thus it seems to have been in the Schubert family. There exists a curious piece of writing by Schubert, dating from 1822, called "My Dream", from which it can clearly be gathered that the young man had suffered under this, and that relations were somewhat strained. It does not make pleasant reading, for reasons of content as well as its curiously stilted and inhibited style. There is an unmistakable ambivalence of feeling towards the authoritarian father, fear of him, and a never-fulfilled yearning to be understood and appreciated. In the Court Chapel and in the hostel attached to it discipline was probably no less severe, and the pupils were certainly not over-fed. An irresistibly charming letter by the fifteen-year-old Franz to his adult brother Ferdinand culminates in an entreaty for a modest contribution to his pocket-money to enable him to buy himself the occasional roll or apple.

One does not hear much about a schoolboy's everyday life. In accordance with the purpose of the institution, the musical training was mainly directed towards proficiency in sight-reading; to this end no more than some elementary theory was required. More than any of the other great masters, Schubert was self-taught. What he learnt from the Court conductor Salieri, who taught him composition when he left the Chapel shortly after his voice had broken, seems to have been confined to the elements of counterpoint and to the techniques most familiar to Salieri, Italian vocal writing. Glancing through one or other of the dusty scores of this master, who was the head of the Vienna Court Chapel for many years, and who owes his place in the history of music mainly to his rivalry with Mozart, one does not find anything but stiff *grandezza* and a very limited style of writing. But at that time the young adept had already gained his spurs. Looking through the considerable amount of music which Schubert wrote at the age of fifteen and sixteen, one feels touched again and again when some turn of melody appears which seems to forecast his peculiar personal language, just as a child's picture may, with softer features, suggest the more marked peculiarities of the adult face we know.

What was said above does not mean that the boy had wasted his time in the Court Chapel and in his school. There is no better training than making good music, and anyone who has grown up in a community where this is a part of the daily routine has learnt something most essential. As well as the service in the Chapel, there were regular orchestral rehearsals in the school, in which he eagerly took part as a violinist, and later as a conductor. He had direct experience of the choir and the orchestra from his early childhood. His youthful works— various kinds of church music, two overtures, his first three symphonies—show that already at that time he had no difficulty whatever in writing scores which corresponded exactly to the desired sound; this ability was derived from an experience which Schumann or Brahms, for instance, who had grown up under less favourable conditions, had to struggle very hard to acquire. The characteristic prominence of trombones in Schubert's orchestral writing has, incidentally, the same source as with Bruckner: three trombones have always been a typical feature of Roman Catholic church music, which was familiar to both from childhood.

Young Schubert left the school connected with the Court Chapel at sixteen and thus renounced his chance of higher education. Biographers originally assumed that he chose the profession of a schoolmaster in order to be exempted from military conscription. This, however, is improbable because, as an official document attests, the adult Schubert measured four feet, eleven inches (1·57 metres) and was thus below the minimum height required for a soldier. After a year at the teachers' training college in Vienna, he entered his father's school as an assistant teacher, charged with giving the youngest children an elementary education.

These are the dry facts behind which, however, more is hidden. The choice of a profession is a decisive act; it is difficult to imagine that Franz Schubert should ever have thought of remaining a schoolmaster all his life. What had become manifest without any possible doubt during his last years at school was his obsession with the urge to create music. His mother had died in 1812. One year later father Schubert entered into a new marriage which again was blessed with children. One must not assume that he was unaware of his son's talent. But as the responsible head of a family he naturally insisted on a safe livelihood. For a boy so crazy about music, but who did not excel as a virtuoso, there was no available musical activity which could have ensured a living. Young Schubert would have had to find patrons, as Beethoven had done from the beginning of his career, or he would have had to struggle and starve like the young Haydn. But since the Austrian state bankruptcy of 1810, generous patrons had become rare, and to live as a needy beggar went against the conscience of a good middle-class family. Another thing must not be forgotten: the custom of hereditary professions at a period of strict class stratification and adherence to one's guild. Father Mozart, conductor of the Archbishop's music at Salzburg, recognised like none other his son's unique gift. But even if Wolfgang had not been more than a middling violinist, he would still have found his way into the Archbishop's band through his father's influence, because to take advantage of one's position in this way was the natural thing to do. By the same custom, the thirteen-year-old Beethoven joined as a harpsichordist the Archbishop of Cologne's music, where his father was a singer. Father Schubert felt comfortable in his teaching job and saw no reason why his son should not be equally satisfied when he set him up in this career. Music was something he could always do in his spare time, as did his older son Ferdinand, who had also become a schoolmaster. And Franz complied.

The decisive circumstance, however, that determined Schubert's career was his nature, and this requires some explanation. He had neither the bearing nor the self-confidence necessary to convince a noble patron of his gifts. Young Beethoven could do this with the proud assurance expressed in his music and the impetuosity with which he asserted himself—

his teacher Haydn called him "the Grand Mogul". Schubert's shortness may possibly have contributed to the fact that from the time of his youth justified pride in his achievements contrasted with a certain shy timidity in his behaviour. His character was not at all equipped for the struggle for existence. Throughout his life and in all its important decisions he preferred to take the line of least resistance. The creative urge that filled his soul seems to have absorbed his entire energy; it looks as if he scrupulously steered clear of any possible conflict by always complying. He saved his strength for the work to which his instinct directed him.

The composer of "Erlkönig" intent upon teaching a horde of obstreperous children the rudiments of reading and writing! A more pointed illustration of "Pegasus yoked" could not easily be found. At that time, in the first year of his enforced drudgery in the school, an event occurred which is unique in the history of music. The young schoolmaster created a new art form: the *Lied*, whose foremost representative he has remained to this day. Some *lieder* written when he was seventeen and eighteen, "Gretchen am Spinnrade" ("Gretchen at the Spinning-Wheel"), "Rastlose Liebe" ("Restless Love"), "Erlkönig" ("Elfking"), are already supreme masterpieces which not even he himself could surpass. But of this event and its background more will be said later.

Every creator is lonely in his work; but some of its reflected splendour will fall on his environment. Schubert had a natural urge for company, and therefore he always found friends who showed interest in his work. It would have been too much to expect them to have had even an inkling of its transcendent glory. But they were his only public, and their appreciation was of value to him.

The *Lied*—it will be explained later why he must rightly be called the creator of this type of composition—stood in the centre of his creative activity from his fifteenth to his twentieth year. He accomplished the task of mastering the innumerable problems inherent in a pioneer venture of this kind by an excess of diligence that combined obsession with perseverance. Glorious achievements such as those mentioned above are still rare in the song harvest of these years, during which he wrote more than three hundred "to exercise his pen", as Brahms said.

How methodically he proceeded can be appreciated if one compares his different settings of the same poem and becomes aware of the consciousness and consistency with which he tackled the problems of declamation, expression and form posed by such a poem, when he had not managed to solve them at the first attempt. And he would always test the result by its live effect. He sang his songs himself—with a weak but expressive voice, as witnesses have reported—or they would be sung by one of his friends, or by a pretty girl from the neighbourhood, Therese Grob, with whom he was in love at that time. And he would improve, transpose, or sometimes write a new setting of the poem if he found that the fault was too deep-rooted. There is no other glimpse into a composer's workshop which reveals, or could reveal, so emphatically all the obstacles on the road to mastery, the gradual progress and the innumerable setbacks. He himself was the most meticulous judge of his work. Later on, when the opportunity for publication arose, only the very best of his output passed his critical scrutiny.

His first "public" success, if such it may be called, came when he had just been installed as an assistant teacher in his father's school. It was a performance of his Mass in F major in the parish church at Lichtental, where he had been baptised seventeen years earlier and where, as a choirboy, he had acquired his first experience of church music. Therese Grob sang the soprano solo, the family and friends were proud of him, and the people of Lichtental were pleased to have such a gifted teacher for their children. The event, and its painfully provincial character, is typical of the circumstances of Schubert's life.

He never did manage to lift himself out of the narrow constriction of his environment and its pernicious effect upon his career. He could create the most magnificent music, but he would have been the last to try to push away the bushel under which his light was hidden.

Schubert's biographers have treated the little romance with the pretty girl from the suburbs with due seriousness. Apart from his youth, an assistant schoolmaster could not have supported a family, and there are no grounds to see more in this affair than a youthful flirtation. In any case Schubert remained a bachelor, and, a few years later, Therese Grob married a master baker. The matter would not be worth mentioning, had it not, in the absence of other subjects of romance, assumed such an annoyingly prominent place in the rank growth of Schubert fiction.

But to return to fact: in the spring of 1816, evidently to improve his material conditions, Schubert applied for the advertised post of music teacher at a teachers' training college in Laibach (now Ljubljana), enclosing a thoroughly dry and non-committal recommendation from Salieri. It is difficult to imagine what would have happened to Schubert in a remote provincial place in the Slovenian borderland. Luckily, Salieri had also supported three other candidates, one of whom obtained the appointment. And Schubert stayed in Vienna. It is symptomatic of his life that he never had any success with an application.

By this time his situation in the school must have already become well-nigh unbearable. His indomitable creative urge had to be confined to moments of leisure, which could hardly be obtained without an occasional neglect of duty. To make matters worse, the young schoolmaster, driven to despair, would occasionally treat his little tormentors with brutality. In fact, the last straw that finally drove him from the school was a row with his father over a sound thrashing he had meted out to a naughty child.

His friends must have seen long before that things could not go on like this. One of them, Franz von Schober, invited him to share his modest quarters, and Schubert left the school. One can only guess at the scenes with his father which must have preceded this step. But his needs were frugal; friend Schober, though not rich, was not without means, and was able to help, and thus Schubert became, and remained to the end of his life, a free artist, something which at that time did not yet exist. With ridiculously small and irregular earnings, always dependent on his friends and patrons, sometimes completely penniless, sometimes almost wealthy for a few weeks on the rare occasions when a somewhat larger fee had just arrived, he was the first bohemian of musical history. He often changed his quarters, and occasionally even had a room of his own. And when he died, the expenses of his burial had to be covered by posthumous publishers' fees.

In the twelve years between his escape from the school in 1816 and his early death, he produced a treasure whose extent alone appears almost incredible. If he was a bohemian, he had the conscientiousness and regular habits of a schoolmaster. He had suffered enough under the yoke of the hated profession to appreciate the freedom to create which he now enjoyed, and to devote all his strength to it. The fervent single-mindedness with which he sat at his work every morning called for some relaxation. This he found in the friendly atmosphere of congenial company. He and his friends made frequent excursions to the nearby Vienna woods; they liked to visit coffee-houses and taverns, and there may occasionally have been some revelry. But the impeccable care bestowed on his work, as well as its enormous mass, contradict the reproach, raised many years later in the memoirs of some of his friends, that he led a slothful life. Undoubtedly they sometimes drank and took it easy: it was not in Schubert's nature to say "no" when friends lured and urged. But the catalogue of his works—he conscientiously put the date on each one he finished, another virtue alongside his meticulously neat handwriting—is the best proof of his irreproachable working discipline.

As mentioned earlier, a great deal of commonplace rubble, piled up in all innocence by Schubert's friends, has to be cleared away. To this end there leads but one reliable path: through his music. It is never without an air of moral superiority that his friends speak of the poor dear fellow who was so gifted and did not get anywhere in the world. Who he really was none of them knew. Never was such a simple, outwardly uneventful life so blessed with extravagantly abundant gifts of creative imagination. It was a double existence in the truest sense of the word. *Schwammerl* to his friends, their little, easy-going drinking-companion, he lived in the transcendental reality of his work, in a region to whose heights no-one was capable of following him. And he would not have been Schubert had he been able to express in words what filled his soul. There are people whose outward lives directly reflect their character, and others who, almost deliberately, present their least essential aspect to the world. This peculiarity is most frequent with the genuine lyricist, whose artistic utterance is the most intimate mirror of his soul, and who therefore, with a certain bashfulness,

hides such feelings when the outside world approaches him.
Grillparzer, with a poet's intuition, grasped at least a shred
of the truth in a poem dedicated to Schubert:

> Lobt ihr mich—es soll mich freuen,
> Schmäht ihr mich—ich muss es dulden.
> Schubert heiss ich, Schubert bin ich,
> mag nicht hindern, kann nicht laden;
> geht ihr gern auf meinen Pfaden,
> nun wohlan, so folget mir!

> (Praise me—and you give me pleasure,
> Spurn me—and I must endure it.
> I am Schubert, and remain it,
> Cannot hinder or entreat you;
> If you wish to tread my pathway,
> Forward then, and follow me!)

At this point it is perhaps necessary to cast a glance at the
Viennese setting with which Schubert's life and work were so
intimately entwined. Of the masters whose names are associated
with the Viennese Classical School, he was the only one who
was actually born there and spent all his life there. All the
others came as immigrants: Haydn from the Burgenland, on
the Hungarian border, to which he returned for many years
as Court Musician to the Prince of Esterhazy, Mozart from
Salzburg, Beethoven from the remote Rhineland. And more
than this: as will be seen later in more detail, Schubert, whose
musical language grew with an almost negligible theoretical
upbringing from his innate genius, stood incomparably closer
to the feeling of the environment from which he stemmed than
all those who had gone through the purifying and in a certain
sense neutralising filter of an orthodox technical training.
Schubert's idiom was the Viennese dialect, which breaks
through in his punctiliously correct written style whenever
everyday matters appear in his letters. And anyone who is
familiar with this down-to-earth yet flexible idiom will detect it,
translated into musical terms, in his melody, and not just in
dance tunes, whose popular background is obvious, but
sometimes in his most sublime utterances.

Vienna is not a city but a world. In its formation popular and cultural forces, landscape and architecture, everyday life and the theatre played their part, just as all kinds of ethnographic influxes from north and south, east and west converged in this centre of a great empire, and were transformed into a homogeneous entity. This may be the reason why Vienna is the only city in the world to have created its own peculiar and unmistakable musical language. But notwithstanding the Viennese waltz and its patron saints, Lanner and Strauss, the most characteristic representative of this language in its highest sense is Schubert, without whom, and without Lanner and Strauss, this language would not have arisen. Only the great individuals are creative in the formation of language. Without Smetana and Dvořák there would be no Czech music, without Glinka, Tchaikovsky and Mussorgsky no Russian music, in spite of all folklore.

Viennese musical culture owes much to the circumstance that for three hundred years talent and love for music were hereditary in the Hapsburg dynasty. The Austrian emperors of the Baroque period were active and by no means incompetent musicians, their Court Chapel was one of the oldest musical institutions in Europe, and the sovereign's interest in music was emulated by the aristocracy. This had a stimulating effect on the whole country, and especially on the capital, Vienna. But up to the end of the eighteenth century it is hardly possible to find anything idiomatic in music that could be called specifically Viennese, and this is true even of certain robust popular tunes of Haydn, which stem rather from the Austrian village with which he had such close ties. Evidently the courtly, aristocratic character of music at that time was still so predominant that popular elements could only penetrate the higher forms of the art in a very marginal way. The breakthrough of these elements did not occur until Schubert's time, with the development of middle-class culture, and he was the first great musician who, as an artist, was fully rooted in this soil.

Vienna has had a turbulent history and has always emerged more or less unscathed from the most dangerous crises and involvements. Perhaps it is from the experience of history that the Viennese have inherited a disinclination to take events or themselves too seriously. In Vienna everything becomes farcical which elsewhere might assume heroic proportions. "Lieber Augustin", a popular comedian at the time of the great plague of 1679, is the historical ancestor of Viennese black humour. His song, "O Du Lieber Augustin", making light of the loss of everything is, ironically, one of the oldest and most popular Viennese folk-songs. From the Turkish siege of 1683, when Vienna, then in desperate straits, was saved in the nick of time by the arrival of a rescuing army, the city has preserved two indestructible mementoes: the *Kipferl*, the favourite break-fast roll in the shape of the Turkish Crescent, and the coffee-house, which an enterprising business-man initiated with sacks of coffee captured from the Turks, and which became an institution without which, to this day, no Viennese could live. And for a century the popular Turkish play remained on the Viennese suburban stage, with Mozart's *Seraglio* as a late example.

At the time of Schubert's childhood Vienna had twice been conquered by the French under Napoleon, but these were already civilised times, and the Vienna bastions, once upon a time able to withstand the Turks, had long fallen into disrepair and were unfit for defence. With the new order established by the Congress of Vienna, the crisis had to some extent been overcome, and in the twenties, when Schubert was at the height of his creative power, the situation was more or less stabilised. This period saw the early flowering of a fast-developing intelligent middle class, who assumed the function which formerly aristocratic patrons had performed and now, in the new century, had almost given up. Admittedly, even wealthy citizens could not afford private orchestras as previously Beethoven's patrons, the Princes Lobkowitz and Lichnovsky, had done; but they did arrange musical evenings, opened their houses on Sundays for gatherings of keen musicians and amateurs, and founded societies such as the *Gesellschaft der Musikfreunde* (Society of Friends of Music), which gave concerts, established a conservatoire, and has to this day remained a centre of musical life in Vienna. It is self-evident that at first none of these new ventures could offer a young musician a livelihood. He was no longer a lackey: he had become a free citizen; but his living depended on chance circumstances. Least of all could he count on an income from his compositions, for, with very scanty protection from copyright, publishing was still at an early stage of development.

Under these circumstances it was fortunate for Schubert that he had a circle of friends who stood by him, found useful contacts for him and, in emergencies, were ready to help as far as their means allowed. The "Schubertians"—each would bring others to the circle—played an important part in Schubert's life and, regrettably, a somewhat dubious one after his death. Several decades later, when asked for information by biographers, many of them wrote down their reminiscences and have thus become the principal source of the Schubert legend, whose philistine one-sidedness has already been touched on.

Franz von Schober, one of his closest friends and the one he seems to have loved best, was the only one who kept silent. He had been the first to offer Schubert an abode; and he thereby helped him extricate himself from the most embarrassing outward crisis of his life. Schober was a restless person. Sometimes he was absent from Vienna for longish periods, but when he was there, Schubert could always have a room in his lodgings. Schober was the life and soul of the group, indefatigable in caring for Schubert, and energetic in taking the initiative when his friend failed to do so himself.

Another faithful follower was Josef von Spaun, who, like Schober, had studied law. Several years his senior, he had already met Schubert at school. He became a civil servant and for many years lived in the provinces, but the two kept in touch. Through Spaun Schubert met the poet Johann Mayrhofer, many of whose poems he set to music and with whom too he became very friendly, at times staying with him. Further members of the circle were the brothers Anselm and Josef Hüttenbrenner, the painter Moritz von Schwind, the poet Eduard von Bauernfeld, the painter Leopold Kupelwieser, and his brother Josef, who wrote the libretto for Schubert's opera *Fierabras*. This remained in his drawer and, like his opera *Alfonso und Estrella*, written to a libretto by Schober, was never performed during his lifetime.

As can be seen, the majority of these young men were actively interested in the arts, and this seems to have been taken for granted among the Schubertians. Schober introduced Schubert to the singer Michael Vogl, who became the most important and most successful performer of his songs. He was a prominent member of the Imperial Opera, the Kärntnertortheater, and at the beginning it was apparently no easy matter to interest him in the shy young beginner. It speaks for his artistic understanding that he took up Schubert's songs so decisively. That this could take place in public only in exceptional cases was due to the practice of the time. Song recitals were unknown; songs were sung at home. With his participation, "Schubertiads" were arranged, musical gatherings in private houses, where Schubert's songs were performed with his friends as the audience. The celebrated singer was an exceedingly self-important gentleman who most probably treated Schubert with dignified condescension. But he did a great deal for him. There is a droll cartoon, probably drawn by Schober, entitled "Michael Vogl and Franz Schubert sally forth to battle and victory", depicting them both: the singer striding majestically in front, his head held high, and Schubert, who hardly comes up to his shoulder, walking modestly three paces behind, with some music under his arm and some more sticking out of his back pocket.

Less pleasant is a statement by the widow of the great singer from which we may conclude that he judged the little man with a curious contempt for his personality: "Vogl was always of the opinion," she writes, "that Schubert was in a somnambulistic state whenever he wrote music. This explains how, in this visionary condition, the scarcely educated boy and later the only moderately educated young man could see into the secrets of life, the emotions, and knowledge." Such is the reward for modesty! It is only regrettable that this nonsense about the simple musician who does not know what he is writing or what is descending on him in his unconscious state of trance was also repeated by other friends and has never ceased to haunt the literature on Schubert. It is a warning that even with contemporary sources one can never be wary enough.

Inseparable from the life of the Schubertians is the local background. Old Vienna, still far from being a large city, must have been enchanting. The inner town with its narrow streets, churches and palaces, the old bastions and the green

belt of the glacis, the extensive view to the heights of the
Vienna woods, the charming, vine-clad surroundings, were
often described by contemporaries, perhaps most feelingly by
Schumann, when he speaks with rapture of Schubert's Great
Symphony which he had discovered there:

> Truly, this Vienna with its St Stephen's spire, its beautiful
> women, its public splendour, and the way it extends, girded
> by the Danube with innumerable ribbons, into the blossom-
> ing plain which gradually rises to higher and higher moun-
> tains; this Vienna, with all its memories of the greatest
> German masters, must be fertile soil for a musician's creative
> imagination. . . . Put the pictures of the Danube, the spire
> of St Stephen's and the far-off Alps together, overlaid with
> a faint catholic fragrance of incense, and you have a picture
> of Vienna! And with this enchanting landscape before us,
> strings may be set vibrating in us which otherwise might
> never have sounded.

It would be wrong not to admit something else which so
directly harmonises with the charm of the town and its environment: Viennese philistinism is a fact, and the Schubertians
were undoubtedly Phaeacians, or *Biedermeier*, as the philistine
Viennese citizen was actually nicknamed in humorous literature
of the time, long before this term indicated a distinct style.
The paradox is that this idyll could exist under a vehemently
reactionary regime. It was the time of state prisons, censorship
and police informers, a time when no correspondence could be
private, because the police opened any letter whose writer or
addressee was suspect, and every person was suspect who at any
time might have been guilty of uttering an irreverent word
against the regime or the church. Count Sedlnitzky, the chief
of police, was the most important functionary of the state, and
the chancellor, Prince Metternich, though a gentleman, was
convinced that a citizen is only reliable as long as he has no
opportunity to form his own opinion. The only mitigating
factor in this form of government was that the executive had
its human weaknesses. The epigram "in Austria reigns crass
absolutism, alleviated by slovenliness" was coined much later,
but was undoubtedly appropriate for the time of the Holy
Alliance.

In such circumstances a thinking man will become a revolutionary or an epicurean. The intellectual élite in Paris always tended towards the first alternative; one only needs to recall the same situation in France, with personalities such as La Fayette, Victor Hugo, or Lamartine. Against such forceful intellects an absolutist regime found itself on the defensive. The performance of Victor Hugo's overtly tendentious plays could be prohibited, but an author of such standing could not be silenced. In Vienna things were different. There the intelligentsia remained politically inconspicuous. Grillparzer suffered in silence and only gave vent to his rancour in posthumous autobiographical writings; Raimund escaped into a fairytale-world of fantasy; and Nestroy confined himself to occasional sarcastic innuendoes. As for the Schubertians, who after all belonged to the enlightened middle class, there is no evidence that any of them uttered a single word of opposition. They were and remained *Biedermeier*. They lived as well as they could afford, and preferably a little better, and did not worry about things which could apparently not be altered. Schubert's friend Mayrhofer was a diligent employee of the Censorship Department, and no one would have thought of this as in any way tainting his honour. Many years later Bauernfeld dedicated to this austere friend a few jocular lines:

> Aged men were his companions,
> Philistines and civil servants,
> One of these, he censored books,
> The strictest too, so we are told.

As an illustration of the prevailing conditions, it is worth mentioning that at a merry gathering of the young friends one of the Schubertians, the law student Johann Chrysostomus Senn, was arrested by the police, and the "assistant schoolmaster Schubert" is mentioned in the police report as having been arrested with him. Schubert was released the next morning; but Senn, of whose supposed political activities nothing can be found, remained in prison for fourteen months, and his career was ruined.

The only one who could open his mouth without restraint in Vienna during the twenties was Beethoven. But he was famous, and known to be a harmless eccentric, and the authorities left him alone. Schubert had from the time of his childhood been used to paternal and governmental authority; he was completely immersed in his work and preferred not to make the ever-present oppression even more painful by resisting it. The term "escapism" is of more recent origin, but it fits to perfection this facet of the Viennese character and the Viennese tendency to turn tragic events into burlesque. After the savagely oppressed revolution of 1848 Nestroy wrote a farce entitled *Freiheit in Krähwinkel* (Freedom in Crowhole), in which a town clerk named Reaction Noble, his deputies Seal and Wax, and the journalist Ultra play important parts, and the last mentioned takes the liberty of remarking: "Censorship is the younger of two terrible sisters; the elder is called Inquisition." Elsewhere a good citizen says: "I don't often think, except when they drag me to it by the hair."

When in 1867, at the time of the worst financial crisis following defeat in the war against Prussia, "The Blue Danube", the most famous of all waltzes, appeared, Johann Strauss simultaneously published a version for male chorus whose original text contains the following doggerel:

> However bad the finances,
> Let's have dances,
> Let's resist these times!
> (Sadly)—O Lord, these times!—
> Let's oppose this plight!
> —Yes, that's clever and right!—
> What's the use of regrets and fears,
> Gaiety is better than tears!

To see the Viennese soul in the melody to which these words were concocted is to commit the pardonable error of seeing the Viennese as they themselves have always liked to appear. What Schubert's music tells us is incomparably nearer to the truth; it is sometimes bright, but rarely jolly, and something pensive and melancholy always seems to be lying hidden beneath the surface. Valid objections can be raised against escapism, but not for anything in the world would one want to renounce Schubert's music which blossomed from it, those carefree, easy-going movements in which the environment, the enchanting landscape is mirrored with such immediacy, and in which, again and again, new melodies appear, reaching a peak of emotion which cannot be expressed in words, or only very inadequately in such terms as: "Life may be happy or sad, but it is unspeakably beautiful."

I have, by the way, a suspicion that there exists something like a language barrier. This seems to be the only possible explanation for the fact that those pieces in which the music not only suggests the local background, but breaks spontaneously into the vernacular (such as the "Trout" Quintet, the last movements of the Octet, the String Quartet in A minor, the two Piano Trios and the Piano Sonata in D major) have over and over again aroused annoyance and disdainful rejection. It is also this kind of music which offers difficulties to the "foreign" performer, because he does not understand the peculiar freedom of articulation which is at least as important for this music as the right speed, although this too is often enough misunderstood. Much the same applies to all really idiomatic music, for example that of Chopin. But his style was made so familiar to virtuosos by the composer himself, as the ideal interpreter, that it could never be forgotten thereafter. With Schubert deplorable distortions still occur. They concern peculiarities of rhythm and phrasing too subtle to be expressed in the written notes, which can never be more than an approximation. Schubert's phrase cannot stand the restriction of a stiff collar. By a four-square rhythmical pedantry this music is as gravely injured and falsified as Raimund's Viennese dialect poetry would be if one were to pronounce the vowels the way he, in the absence of a more precise notation, wrote them.

The chronicle of Schubert's life during the twelve years in which he could freely devote himself to his creative work is poor in external events. It was rare enough for his name to appear in public, and when, gradually, some of his works found publishers and were printed, they were at best accepted with respect or with the condescending acknowledgment that here was a promising talent. The first successful attempt to have his music published is described in an account by Leopold von Sonnleithner, a Viennese lawyer. Leopold's father,

B

Ignaz von Sonnleithner, regularly arranged musical evenings in his house, at which even orchestral works were played, and Schubert's songs, especially "Erlkönig", "Der Wanderer", and "Gretchen am Spinnrade", were received with exceptional interest. Leopold writes:

> I offered "Erlkönig" to the music dealers Tobias Haslinger and Anton Diabelli, but both refused to publish it—even without a fee—because, since the composer was unknown and the piano accompaniment too difficult, successful sales could not be expected. Hurt by this refusal, we decided to have the songs published for Schubert's own benefit. I myself, Hüttenbrenner, and two other patrons of the arts put down the money for the first one and had "Erlkönig" engraved in February 1821. When at a musical soirée in our house my father announced that "Erlkönig" was now available, about a hundred copies were bought there and then by those present, and the costs of the second publication were covered. Thus we had the first twelve pieces engraved at our expense, and Diabelli sold them on commission. Out of the ample proceeds we paid Schubert's arrears in rent, his debts to the shoemaker, the tailor, the restaurant and the coffee-house, and could still hand over to him a considerable sum of money. Unfortunately he needed such tutelage, for he had no sense at all of domestic economy.

When Schubert later sold the engraved plates of these works, all of them songs, to the publisher Diabelli, who now showed interest in them, his friends found this very rash. However, this was one of the rare opportunities in his life to have some money in his pocket. Otherwise the publishers were cautious and were interested almost exclusively in music which, under the prevailing conditions, promised safe sales—songs, piano compositions for two and four hands, and dances. Nevertheless, there were some private commissions. To these we owe the "Trout" Quintet and the Octet, which, however, as already mentioned, had to wait a long time before they were published. The only one of his string quartets to appear in print during his lifetime, the Quartet in A minor, was greeted by the Leipzig *Allgemeine musikalische Zeitung* with the laconic comment: "As a first attempt it is not to be despised." It was his thirteenth.

To have larger-scale works published was no easy matter. Schubert would not have been Viennese had he not been interested in the theatre; and at a time when Rossini's star was rising to its zenith and Weber's *Freischütz* was enjoying a sensational success, it was the natural thing for a young composer to think about opera. His first operatic attempt, though, dates from before this time. It was called *Des Teufels Lustschloss* (The Devil's Country Palace) and was already finished when he took up his teaching post in 1814. His last opera *Der Graf von Gleichen* (The Count of Gleichen) remained a sketch at his death. He left a dozen operas and operatic fragments and saw only one of them on the stage, the one act singspiel *Die Zwillings-brüder* (The Twin Brothers), which, thanks to the efforts of Vogl, who sang the leading part in it, was performed at the Kärntner-tortheater in June 1820. In the programme the work is called "Farcical comedy with music". Judging from a report in the Leipzig *Allgemeine musikalische Zeitung*, the Schubertians must have made a collective appearance on this occasion: "That Herr Schubert has many friends who are also very active in promoting him was evident at the first performance. But these may have forgotten that between *fiasco* and *furore*, as the Italians say, there is a tremendous difference, that for the beginner friendly encouragement is the finest, most beneficial reward, and that here as everywhere the middle way is probably always the best." Its reception did not amount to much more than polite recognition, and the work soon disappeared from the repertoire.

One year later the situation became even more difficult for a local composer, since the Italian impresario Barbaja, who became the director of the Kärntnertortheater, also had La Scala in Milan and the Teatro San Carlo in Naples in his hands. This meant a flood of Italian operas in Vienna (with famous singers, and a personal visit by Rossini, who was tempestuously acclaimed) and hard times for German opera, which in any case led a Cinderella existence. Barbaja was clever enough to commission a new opera from the most popular operatic composer in Germany, Weber. The result was *Euryanthe*, first performed with great splendour in October 1823; its success, however, lagged far behind *Der Freischütz*.

Schubert, who at a personal meeting with Weber could not hide his disappointment with the new work, thus forfeited the goodwill of his famous colleague, who, as director of the Dresden opera, might have been a great help to him. Weber rejected *Alfonso und Estrella*, the opera whose libretto, an inflated romantic affair, stemmed from Schober. And Schubert's recently finished opera *Fierabras* and his singspiel *Die Verschworenen* (The Conspirators), written in the same year, were likewise discarded. The latter is the only one of Schubert's operas which is theatrically effective, and it has often been successfully performed, though never in Schubert's lifetime. It has, apart from its irresistibly fresh music, the advantage of an amusing, well-built libretto, whose subject was borrowed by the author, Ignaz Castelli, from Aristophanes's comedy *Lysistrata*. This singspiel has the disadvantage of most one-act operas, namely that it is not easy to find the right work to complete the bill; but this difficulty should not be insuperable.

In a letter to Leopold Kupelwieser, Schubert complains about his operatic misfortunes. "The opera *Fierabras* by your brother[1] (who acted unwisely in leaving the theatre) was declared unusable and hence my music was not required either. Castelli's opera *Die Verschworenen*, set to music by a Berlin composer, has been received with acclaim there. So I would again appear to have written two operas in vain."

As a symptom of contemporary conditions it may be mentioned that, if *Die Verschworenen* had been performed in Vienna, it would not have been allowed to keep its title. As with all his operas, Schubert had dutifully submitted it to the censor. The result was that the content was passed, but the title rejected. The story could not be more harmless. The conspirators are a group of wives who, by strike action, want to force their husbands, returning from a crusade—without the Middle Ages there could be no opera—to swear that in future they will stay at home. This is answered by the husbands, who have had wind of it, with a counter-strike. There are strike breakers, comical entanglements and a happy end. But in Austria it was not permitted to speak of conspirators. It sounded risky and smacked of politics. Therefore the opera was renamed

[1] Joseph Kupelwieser, the author of the libretto, had been secretary at the Kärntnertortheater.

Der häusliche Krieg (Domestic War), and this is still its sub-title.

Two plays to which Schubert wrote incidental music, *Die Zauberharfe* (The Magic Harp) (1820) and *Rosamunde* (1823) were performed at the popular Theater an der Wien, but both were failures. Judging from the fragments of text preserved with Schubert's music, which consists of entr'actes, ballet scenes, choruses and melodrama, there is no need to shed any tears over the loss of these plays. The author of *Die Zauberharfe*, Georg von Hofmann, had, a few months earlier, produced the libretto to Schubert's opera *Die Zwillingsbrüder*. The romantic drama *Rosamunde* was by Helmine von Chézy, the authoress of Weber's *Euryanthe*, which has preserved her name for posterity. From what we can deduce from synopses in newspaper reports, *Rosamunde* must have been an even more pitiful concoction than the wretched *Euryanthe*, which many, in order to save the music, have tried to improve, but without being able to cure its defects. For the performance Schubert used the overture he had written for *Alfonso und Estrella*. Later he replaced it by the overture to *Die Zauberharfe*, and this overture was published in 1827 in a version for piano duet under the title "Overture to Rosamunde", which it has kept ever since.

As it is always amusing to hear something about the manners and customs of earlier times, we may insert here what Wilhelm von Chézy, the son of the poetess, tells us of the performance, in which Madame Katharina Vogel, wife of the director of the Theater an der Wien, played a leading part:

> The husband was as insignificant and meagre as his wife was corpulent and imposing, he a withered gatepost, she a great barrel. On the stage, where she played maturer parts with great skill, she still looked very fine, of course with the aid of well known means, one of which was truly heroic. I have more than once watched it being applied in the theatre dressing room. The great barrel put on a corset of the strongest drill, with steel splints, strong whalebone, reinforced eyelets and new cords of the strongest hemp twine which were drawn together by two stalwart houseboys. When the two thickset Austrians pulled the corset together with all their might, each stemming his knee against her enormous hip, it seemed as though one were looking at a

torture chamber and a witch. It did, in fact, require some witchcraft for this cruelly constrained mass to breathe, move and speak, which she managed to do quite reasonably.

The unfortunate *Rosamunde* had only two performances, and Schubert, who was ailing—this will be discussed later—was presumably not present.

The disappointments which he experienced with his stage works probably contributed to the depression which is frequently noticeable in his letters of these years. The main reason for their failure is evidently to be found in the absurdity of the libretti he set to music. The fact is that he knew nothing of the exigencies of the theatre, that the average German dramatic writing of his time was unimaginably pitiful, and that he was far too uncritical with regard to the texts he accepted, quite apart from the atrocious operatic poetry which a composer had to put up with. Mayrhofer was a gifted, ambitious poet, but the following lines from his singspiel *Die Freunde von Salamanca* (The Friends of Salamanca), set to music by the eighteen-year-old Schubert, are an example of what even he regarded as permissible in an opera:

> The shepherd, by the silver stream,
> Beneath the greenwood's leafy tent,
> Of his fair love doth sit and dream
> And yearning sings his sad lament.

The irresistible tune to these words has survived; Schubert used it, nine years later, in his Octet as a theme with variations.

His ever ready imagination plunged with wonderful unconcern into any venture that suited his creative impulse. It is almost unbelievable that the harvest of that year 1823 contains, beside the two above-mentioned operas and the music to *Rosamunde*, more than a dozen glorious songs—"Du bist die Ruh" is among them—a large quantity of piano music and the great song cycle *Die schöne Müllerin*. Mayrhofer, who wrote two librettos for him, was many things, but not a dramatist; Schober and Kupelwieser were well-educated amateurs; Madame Chézy less than that; and Bauernfeld, the author of Schubert's last opera *Der Graf von Gleichen*, though in later life a successful playwright, was at that time only a beginner. With *Der Graf von Gleichen*, by the way, a snag arose right at the beginning because the censor objected to it. The hero was a proverbial bigamist, and such things were not allowed on the Austrian stage.

The most original personality of the Viennese popular theatre, Ferdinand Raimund, unfortunately never had any artistic dealings with Schubert. The only occasion when they are known to have met, and probably as strangers, was Beethoven's funeral, at which they both acted as torch-bearers. They were in many respects kindred spirits, and not only through the common background of the town in which they lived and worked. Both were rooted in the fantasy world of romanticism, and both found it difficult to force the abundant riches of their vision into a concise form. There is more of Raimund in Schubert and more of Schubert in Raimund than one might suspect. And Raimund too was misjudged; the poet disappeared behind the popular actor. At that time Grillparzer, despite the fact that he had aesthetically little in common with him, was probably the only one who understood that under the rubble of Raimund's language—so expressive in the dialect but always somehow stilted and restricted in Standard German —a true poet lay hidden. With a play by Raimund and music by Schubert an immortal work might have resulted; this too belongs to the unfulfilled possibilities which accompanied Schubert's life.

It is similarly symbolic that the only documented occasion when he crossed Beethoven's path was at the above-mentioned funeral. He worshipped the great man, but shyly and from a distance. Anton Schindler, Beethoven's factotum and first biographer, who was also associated with the Schubert circle, claims that on his death-bed the master read Schubert's songs with interest and appreciation. But there are no other witnesses for this assertion, and there are statements by Schindler elsewhere which are not altogether reliable. In any case, these two, who, seen from our distance, soar at an unattainable height above their time, never had any personal relations with each other.

Schubert rarely left Vienna. He spent two summer holidays, which were extended until the autumn, in Zseliz in West

Hungary on the estate of Count Esterházy, to whose daughters, Marie and Caroline, he gave piano lessons. Several of his friends, among them Bauernfeld, who wrote a humorous poem about it, maintained that the younger one of his pupils, Caroline, had been the object of his adoration. Apart from the love affair with Therese Grob, this is the only tender inclination that has been attributed to him. But when one considers Schubert's personality and the immeasurable social distance between a countess and a poor musician, it becomes difficult to take the story seriously. One could sooner believe in an affair with a pretty chambermaid in Zseliz whom he mentions in one of his letters. His words suggest that he belonged more or less to the servants there, and that he felt uncomfortable and lonely.

His pen, however, was never idle. To his second stay in Zseliz we owe, among other things, two of his most important works for piano duet, presumably written for his aristocratic pupils: the Duo in C major (which has been taken by Schumann and others, though probably wrongly, to be the sketch for a lost symphony) and the *Divertissement à l'Hongroise*, which, with its Hungarian rhythms and melodies, pays homage to the *genius loci*.

But what he writes to his brother Ferdinand sounds rather depressed:

. . . Lest these lines should mislead you into supposing that I am unwell or not in the best of spirits, I hasten to assure you of the contrary. That happy time has, of course, passed, when every object was surrounded by a youthful glory; now instead there is the odious recognition of miserable reality, which (thank God!) I try to improve as far as possible by the exercise of my imagination. We suppose that happiness attaches to any place where we were once happy, whereas it is only within ourselves, and so I was at first disappointed here—a repetition of the experience I had before at Steyr; but I am now better able to find happiness and tranquillity within myself than I was then.

And to Schober he writes (21 September 1824):

. . . Here I am, all alone, in the depths of Hungary, where I have unfortunately allowed myself to be lured for a second time, without having a single person with whom I could exchange an intelligent word. Since the time when you left, I have hardly written any songs but have worked at various instrumental things. Heaven alone knows what is going to happen to my operas. Although I have been in good health again for the last five months, the absence of you and Kupel often lowers my spirits, and my days are sometimes very miserable. . . .

More stimulating than his stay in Zseliz were occasional trips to the Austrian provinces, to Graz, where Anselm Hütten-brenner had become musical director, to Linz, Spaun's home town, or to Steyr, the home of Michael Vogl. A longer trip, which he undertook in the summer of 1825 together with Vogl, brought him to Steyr, Linz, Gmunden, Salzburg and Gastein. With his sociable nature and his need for company he found friendly personal contacts everywhere, and he reports animatedly on his experiences in letters to his family. From his utterances it may be discerned that he had no liking for the clericalism which was part and parcel of the Austrian system of government, and growing up during the heroic era of the Napoleonic wars had evidently made him a pacifist. He writes vividly, and when he decribes how he performed his songs with Vogl one notices the artistic satisfaction this partner offered him; one may also gather how rarely he was permitted to enjoy the pleasure of feeling the immediate impact of his music and of being a little spoiled by personal friends and by admirers of his work. These reports on his journeys are Schubert's most attractive letters:

[12 September, 1825] . . . Vogl sang some songs of mine, whereupon we were invited for the following evening and asked to do our stuff before a select assembly. The music made a great impression, especially the Ave Maria mentioned in my first letter. The way Vogl sings and I accompany him, so that at such moments we seem to be *one*, is something quite new and unprecedented for these people. . . .

[Steyr, 21 September] . . . After a few hours we arrived at

the quaint, but extremely dirty and disgusting town of Hallein. . . . It was impossible to persuade Vogl to visit the salt mines; his mighty spirit, spurred on by gout, was striving towards Gastein like a traveller towards a spark of light on some murky night. So we drove on past Golling, from where we could already see the first high, impassable mountains whose fearsome gorges are traversed by the Lueg Pass. Having slowly clambered up a high mountain, with other terrible mountains towering in front of our noses and on either side, as though it were the end of the world, we reached the top and suddenly found ourselves looking down into a frightful gorge, so that for a moment our hearts were on the point of stopping. . . . Amid this dreadful scenery, man has tried to perpetuate his even more dreadful bestiality. For it was here that the Bavarians on one side of the Salzach which forges its way far far below, and the Tyroleans on the other, perpetrated that horrible slaughter: the Tyroleans, hidden among the rocky peaks, fired down with devilish glee on the Bavarians who were trying to capture the pass, and those who were hit hurtled down into the depths without ever knowing where the shots had come from. This most shameful beginning, which was continued for several days and weeks, is commemorated by a chapel on the Bavarian side and a red cross in the cliffs on the Tyrolean side, partly to mark the spot and partly, through these sacred symbols, as an atonement. Thou glorious Christ! To what abominations must Thou lend Thine image! Thou Thyself, the most gruesome monument to human depravity, they set up Thine image as if to say: "Behold, with our insolent feet we have trampled upon almighty God's most perfect creation, and should we then shrink from light-heartedly destroying the vermin we call man?" . . .

In the summer of 1823 the most fateful event of his life occurred, one which permanently damaged his health. A remark in one of the letters to Schober quoted above alludes to it. From all the existing reports it must be assumed that it was a venereal infection, most probably syphilis, for which, with the state of medical knowledge at that time there were only very dubious methods of treatment. His condition forced him to stay in hospital repeatedly. A large part of *Die schöne Müllerin* was written in the infirmary; his creative activity knew no rest. The above-mentioned memoirs of Wilhelm von Chézy, which Kreissle quotes in his biography, show unequivocally that the nature of his illness was no secret to his friends. A few excerpts from letters may shed some light on the course of this dark episode:

[Schubert to Schober, 14 August 1823]: I feel fairly well. Whether I shall ever become completely healthy again, I almost doubt.

[Schwind to Schober, 26 December 1823]: Schubert is better. It should not be long before he is able to wear his own hair again, which had to be shaved off because of the rash. He is wearing a very nice wig.

[Schwind to Schober, 22 February 1824]: Schubert is fine. He has abandoned his wig and is growing sweet little curls.

[Schwind to Schober, 6 March 1824]: Schubert is now much better. He says that after a few days of the new treatment he felt that the back of the illness had been broken and everything was different.

No wonder that Schubert's letters contain melancholy utterances:

[Schubert to Leopold Kupelwieser, 31 March 1824]: In a word, I feel myself to be the unhappiest, most miserable being in the world. Imagine a man whose health will never be right again, and who in his despair makes things worse and worse instead of better. Imagine a man, I say, whose brightest hopes have been shattered, to whom the happiness of love and friendship offers at best pain, who is in danger of losing his enthusiasm (at least when it is stimulating) for all things beautiful, and ask yourself whether this is not an unhappy, miserable man?

The miracle is that in his music the bright sun again and

again breaks through; in spite of everything his imagination could overcome reality.

What he never found was a permanent abode. As already mentioned, he was put up by various friends in turn; sometimes he could rent a room of his own; and then again, when all else failed, it happened that he would stay with his parents in the suburb Rossau, where his father now had his school. One can only hope that his strictness did not make the prodigal son's life even harder than it already was. There was no regular job to be found. When in 1826, after Salieri's death, his deputy Eybler moved up to the top position, Schubert applied for the vacant post of Deputy Court Conductor. But he failed; a light-opera composer, Josef Weigl, was appointed. And when in the same year a conductorship at the Kärntnertortheater fell vacant, it went to Schubert's friend Franz Lachner.

At the beginning of 1828 there were the beginnings of an improvement in his circumstances. His songs were becoming more widely known, German publishers were beginning to show an interest in his music, and Schubert was induced by his friends to give a public recital of his works. It was his first and last. As was customary, the programme was very varied. Apart from choral works and songs, sung by Michael Vogl and Ludwig Tietze, another successful performer, it contained the Piano Trio in E flat and the first movement of the new String Quartet in G major—to present the public with the whole of this extensive work was more than he dared. Schubert's supporters could easily fill a hall, and the undertaking was both artistically and financially a great success. Schubert felt immensely rich and, a few days later, took some of his friends to a recital by Paganini, the most sensational event of the season, behind which his own modest public venture almost disappeared.

It was again a year of colossal productivity. Its harvest was the Great Symphony in C major, the String Quintet, the Fantasy in F minor for piano duet, his last three great piano sonatas, the fourteen songs which after his death were pubished under the title *Schwanengesang* (Swan Song), the extraordinary choral work *Miriams Siegesgesang* (Miriam's Song of Triumph) to a poem by Grillparzer, and his last and greatest mass, the one in E flat.

We know little of the summer which, owing to lack of funds,

he spent in Vienna. In September he moved to his brother Ferdinand's. At that time he had the opportunity of studying the English complete edition of Handel's works, which impressed him deeply and may have contributed to his decision to take up serious studies in counterpoint. And he did, in fact, get in touch with an esteemed theoretician, the court organist Simon Sechter who, a quarter of a century later, was to become Bruckner's teacher. Regular lessons were arranged but after the first one, at the beginning of November, Schubert fell ill with acute symptoms of the digestive tract. It is assumed that it was a case of typhoid fever, which at that time was endemic in Vienna. This is his last letter to Schober, written on 12 November 1828:

> I am ill. For the last eleven days I have had nothing to eat or drink; I can only totter feebly from my armchair to my bed and back. Rinna is treating me. If I do take any nourishment my body rejects it immediately. Please would you be so kind as to let me have some books to help me in this desperate situation. Those of Cooper's I have read are *The Last of the Mohicans*, *The Spy*, *The Pilot*, and *The Pioneers*. If by any chance you have anything else by him, I implore you to deposit it for me with Frau von Bogner at the coffee-house. My brother, who is conscientiousness itself, will be the most reliable person to bring it to me. Or something else instead.

Ferdinand and his wife and Schubert's young half-sister Josefa nursed him. He died on 19 November. The shattered state of his health may have contributed to the fatal issue of his illness.

If there is anything at all that could reconcile us to the atrociousness of this catastrophe, to this early extinction of a source of beauty, richer and more abundant than any before, it would be the thought that this short, acute illness may perhaps have preserved a poor suffering body from an even crueller fate—that of Donizetti, Smetana, Wolf or Nietzsche, with whom the malignant disease that had afflicted Schubert some years earlier resulted in agonising torture and mental decay.

2

MELODY

CIVILISED MAN, LIVING in a world riddled with artificiality, is in danger of forgetting primary phenomena. In our day it seems necessary to point out that melody is such a primary phenomenon, and that there has never been a period in history when melody was not the essence of what people considered to be music.

A history of melody would fill volumes. At all times and in all cultural periods it has had its own specific forms of expression, and they have left their traces behind like geological deposits in rock. Music could never have become a highly developed art, had it not arrived at the subtlest means of expression over and above that primary phenomenon, but melody has always offered to music, as the earth did to Antaeus, an unshakeable foundation from which it could gather strength.

The history of music shows a certain periodicity. Again and again there has been highly developed technical sophistication, followed by reaction against such sophistication, with an endeavour to return to the primary element, melody. Such a reaction against the polyphony of baroque music, with Bach as its greatest exponent, led by way of the graceful simplicity of rococo style to the formal perfection of the Viennese classics, to Haydn and Mozart, young Schubert's point of departure. As already mentioned, he was essentially self-taught. But he grew up at a period of exceptionally mature style; in this situation a gifted beginner could learn more from his great predecessors than from mediocre teachers. One of these, Wenzel Ruzitska, who gave him lessons in harmony, put it in a nutshell when he later declared that he had nothing to teach him, for "he's learnt it all from God".

How little he could gain from Salieri, for whom the Viennese classical symphony was a foreign world, and who always earnestly warned him not to waste his time with such a fruitless pursuit as writing German songs, is obvious enough. As a pupil of Gluck, Salieri had chosen a different path from his more

successful compatriots Cimarosa and Paisiello. He had nothing
of the traditional ease and fluency of Italian melody. What he
could teach Schubert was at best its formalism. And Beethoven,
who after his studies of strict counterpoint with Haydn and
Albrechtsberger had come to Salieri for a short time to get an
idea of the gentle art of Italian vocal writing—the duet
"O namenlose Freude" ("O joy, o joy beyond expressing") in
Fidelio is based upon an exercise he wrote for Salieri—remained
an uncanny figure for him. When in 1816 Schubert took part
in a jubilee celebration in honour of his teacher, he wrote in his
diary the following note, which clearly echoes views he had
often heard expressed by Salieri. It is not hard to guess that
the innuendo is aimed at Beethoven:

It must be beautiful and refreshing for an artist to see all his
pupils gathered about him, each one striving to give of his
best for his jubilee, and to hear in all these compositions the
expression of pure beauty, free from all the eccentricity that
is common among most composers nowadays and is due
almost wholly to one of our greatest German artists; that
eccentricity which joins and confuses the tragic with the
comic, the agreeable with the repulsive, heroism with
howlings and the holiest with harlequinades, without
distinction, so as to goad people to madness instead of lifting
them up to God. To see this eccentricity banished from the
circle of his disciples, and instead to look upon pure, holy
nature, must be the greatest pleasure for an artist who,
guided by such a one as Gluck, learned to know nature and
to uphold it in spite of the unnatural conditions of our age.[1]

This sounds disarmingly naïve for a nineteen-year-old. He
revised his judgment on Beethoven soon enough, and perhaps
his view of Salieri as well. But in the instrumental works of his
youth, the symphonies, overtures, sonatas and string quartets
he wrote before he was nineteen, there is as yet hardly any
trace of Beethoven as a model. He followed the more familiar
language of Haydn and Mozart. That the simple, dignified
melodic style of Gluck was also an influence is hinted at in the

[1] Quoted from *Franz Schubert: a Documentary Biography* by O. E. Deutsch,
translated by Eric Blom, London, 1955.

above note. But like all the great masters Schubert, too, had to find his own way to melody. Theoreticians have always fought shy of such slippery ground. In traditional counterpoint there can be found elements of a theory of melody, but beyond this the treatises of all times have kept silent. They were right to do so, for melody is the very essence of invention, of the creative act, and if this is lacking, no theory will help.

Schubert's individual melodic idiom manifested itself early on. It is already noticeable in his first symphonies wherever melody comes directly to the fore, in the second subject of an allegro, in idyllic andante or allegretto movements (this is where we most feel the real Schubert), whereas fast, energetic movements still reveal their descent from other sources, and all too often owe their existence to casual improvisation. The young composer had not yet learnt to wait for the inspiration which was worth writing down. This is a typical feature of juvenility. With the enormous increase in music consumption in our century, created by the demands of public performance, radio, and gramophone records, even such early efforts have met with increasing appreciation, but this does not alter the fact that they are immature. Schubert was by nature a lyricist. The epic, dynamic component of symphonic style was not in his immediate grasp and had to wait for a later phase of his development. Like the specifically dynamic character of true instrumental style, the element of polyphony was basically alien to his nature. His first mass, in F major, with which the young assistant teacher introduced himself at the parish church in Lichtenthal, is most impressive in its lyrical sections, the *Kyrie* and *Benedictus*. Behind his religious lyricism the gentle, optimistic piety of Haydn is unmistakably present. A letter about his religious music which Schubert wrote many years later is indicative of his attitude:

[To his family, 25 July 1825] . . . Everyone was struck by the piety I have expressed in a hymn to the holy Virgin [Ave Maria]; this seems to affect every heart and to inspire devotion. I think the reason is that I never force myself to devotion and never write such hymns or prayers unless such a feeling overwhelms me spontaneously; but then it is usually genuine, true devotion. . . .

This already holds true of the young composer of the Mass in F major. In fast, energetic movements he had at that time not yet found his own style, and when, following tradition, he writes a fugue (in the *Cum sancto spiritu*), he becomes conventional; he took his lead from what he was accustomed to hearing in church. In the two masses he wrote in the following year he does not show any significant progress in this respect. The *Hosanna* fugue in the otherwise purely lyrical, extraordinarily attractive Mass in G major, and the dutifully fugal *Cum sancto spiritu* in the Mass in B flat are the weakest episodes in these works. At a later stage he found his personal style of polyphony, his expressive melody of inner parts, but that took time.

There is more than one reason why Schubert, the scion of the Vienna suburbs, the untaught, the early romantic, initially found in melody all he needed. In his generation two epochs overlap. During the first quarter of the nineteenth century Beethoven's maturity, the apex of classicism, coincides with the first breakthrough of the romantic spirit in the music of Weber and Schubert. The romantic movement turned the artist towards a psychological borderland, to a search for heightened means of expression in a sphere where dark, chaotic forces hold sway. Schubert's *Winterreise* and his late settings of Heine poems point in this direction. Beethoven's exalted sense of form, matured to the highest spirituality in his last works, is opposed by the romantic overflow of feeling where form tends to be felt rather as an inhibition. It is no accident that at the same time the ageing Goethe, with his unshakably classical form-consciousness, was offering sceptical resistance to the rising tide of romanticism; such antagonism manifests itself much more openly in literature than in the more instinctive reactions of the musician.

Young Schubert sang as his nature bade him. From the classical symphony he took over what was most congenial to him: melody. He accepted its formal lay-out as far as he was able at that time to comprehend it: as a reliable basis for pleasant symmetry. And he proceeded accordingly without concerning himself with deeper principles of structure which are immanent in classical form but are easily ignored if one is only aware of the surface. What delights one again and again is the freshness of Schubert's melodic invention, and here he touches on the most spontaneous and instinctive mode of popular musical expression.

In the eighteenth century there arose an intense interest in folk art, folk poetry and folk song. In Germany it is linked with the name of the poet Herder who, as we know, exercised a remarkable influence on the young Goethe. This movement, however, was by no means limited to Germany. Large strata of the population had gradually entered into cultural awareness. This had been one of the causes of the French Revolution, which in turn enhanced the contributions of this class to culture at large, so that during the following decades music became a popular art which by its very nature naïvely resisted any formalism. Art music and folk music now had to meet each other half way. At that time in Germany, as already earlier in Italy and France, it was opera which began to attract an ever growing audience. And opera soon adapted its style to a new, still rather raw public. Beside vocal virtuosity, which hitherto had held the greatest appeal for sophisticated audiences, there now came what the naïve listener demanded above all else: melody, easy tunes. This development can be observed most clearly in the French and Italian opera overture. Though at the turn of the century it still had a formal structure, it had by the twenties become a loosely-knit potpourri, a sequence of tunes.

Weber, who as a representative of early romanticism was in some ways akin to Schubert, shows himself to be already moving this way in his overtures, although he still superficially follows the classical form-pattern. At heart he was, like Schubert, a melodist; and *Der Freischütz* (1821), which within one year made him the most popular German composer of his time, owed its success first and foremost to its catchy tunes. Weber calls the bridesmaids' chorus ("The bridal wreath for thee we bind") a "folksong", which does not suggest that he used a traditional tune, but that this melody has the unaffected simplicity of a folksong. Owing to his position as director of the Dresden opera, a theatre with a deeply-rooted Italian tradition, Weber was forced into a situation which makes it understandable that to him Rossini, whose operas were at that time triumphantly carrying all before them, was the arch enemy. For young Schubert, Rossini was an incomparably fascinating phenomenon and his influence on him at that stage of his development is clearly recognisable, particularly in his Sixth Symphony (1817) and in two overtures written during the same year, which later his brother Ferdinand rightly called "Italian". A few years later this threat to his originality had been overcome. The overture to *Rosamunde* (known under this name, though, as already mentioned, it was originally written for *Die Zauberharfe* of 1820) still has the loosely constructed Rossinian lay-out, and in the introduction Schubert even used some fragments from one of these "Italian" overtures; but here every bar already bears the stamp of Schubert's own idiom. Italian opera no longer had anything to offer him.

Stylistically Schubert and Rossini were antipodes, but they had one thing in common: for both melody was the very essence of composition. By then Schubert had already found his way to the German *lied*, and this was the decisive event of his early development. With Rossini Italian opera entered the period of its richest flowering, which extended from him to Donizetti, Bellini and Verdi. What Rossini contributed to it was the impulse of a genius, of a musician of spirit and imagination. For two centuries Italian operatic style had been determined by vocal virtuosity, and this was Rossini's most precious heritage. Gluck despised and resisted it; Mozart made judicious use of it, as he did with any artistic means he found available; with Rossini vocal brilliance reached the climax of its development, and his mode of shaping a melody derived naturally from it. One only needs to compare a Rossini aria with a *lied* by Schubert to see that they belong to two different worlds.

Rossini's richly chiselled melody is still an offshoot of the eighteenth century, of rococo style. The music of this period, like baroque architecture with its lavish ornamentation, displays a characteristic aversion to plain surfaces. To put it in a simple formula, one could say that in this style long notes are inclined to dissolve into ornaments. With this tendency the art of singing developed a rich virtuoso technique. Sequences of simple, long notes were garnished with cascades of brilliant *fioritura*, and gifted singers would improvise lavish additions in order to render their parts even more brilliant. Rossini, determined to curb this abuse, offered still more lavish ornamentation. His passage-work was rich enough to make any unwelcome addition redundant, and thus he offered his singers incomparable material with which to show off their virtuosity.

It is undeniable that vocal coloratura, which like any virtuoso technique has its own appeal, destroys the intimate connection between the words and the musical phrase. Coloratura melody becomes a *solfeggio*; it can be melodically attractive but the words are now no more than meaningless syllables. One can understand that this was completely contrary to Schubert's natural urge for expression.

The eighteenth-century tendency to ornamentation may also have been furthered by the fact that the musician's standard instruments, the clavichord and the harpsichord, could by this means turn a deficiency into an advantage. The deficiency was the short, quickly dying sound of the plucked string. To arrive at a mellifluous and coherent melody one had to break up long notes by ornamentation. Any Bach *sarabande* can show how this was done. And in addition to the ornaments indicated by the composer, the player still made use of his traditional privilege of improvising even richer embellishments, a custom against which C. P. E. Bach already found it necessary to protest. Here, in instrumental style, as well as in vocal style, the result was a kind of instinctive avoidance of long, plain notes and unadorned simple phrases. How much this tendency influenced the style of the period can be seen in classical instrumental music. Here ornamentation is certainly very moderate, compared with the vocal style in opera, but a Haydn or Mozart adagio is rarely without embellishments, and this can in fact be regarded as a general and important feature of late eighteenth-century style.

Beethoven was the first to discard the pigtail of rococo fashion consciously and with conviction. With him, for the first time in more recent musical history, the large, broadly-phrased melody came into its own; it can already be found in such early works as his pianoforte trios Op. 1, his first pianoforte sonatas and violin sonatas, his Septet and his string quartets Op. 18. Renouncing florid ornaments, he achieves the profound expressiveness of his adagios with broad, nobly-shaped melodies. Like him, Schubert found out in his own way how to model an unadorned melody, to let it make its impression solely through its shapely proportions and natural curves, just as the sculptor of antiquity and the Renaissance treated the naked human body. To draw the conclusion from what has been stated: Schubert's melody is the result of a particular historical situation coinciding with a unique specific talent. The time was ripe for absolute melody, melody free from all frills and florid accessories; ripe for the appearance of an artist whose sensibility was rooted in the musical instinct of the people; and ripe for the development of a mode of expression which, in accordance with the needs of listeners without an educated musical background, was able to concentrate everything essential in the shape of a melody. That the time was also ripe for the creation of the *lied* as an art form, an event which was connected in a decisive way with an extra-musical factor, the development of German poetry, will be shown later.

Schubert's melody has peculiarities which can most easily be approached if one takes his maturest inventions as a starting point. In these, apart from idiomatic turns such as can be found in the music of every great composer, we notice three essential features in which he seems superior to even the greatest melodists: the relaxed breadth of phrasing, the variety of rhythmical impulses, and the inexhaustibility of new inventions at every turn of the way. The song "Du bist die Ruh" may be taken as an example. It begins with almost cool restraint, with a shapely melody which has the smooth beauty of marble. Eight short lines of Rückert's poem tend to evolve, as one might expect, into a symmetrical sixteen-bar phrase which, after the fourteenth, seems to be ready for a simple conclusion. But instead of this something unexpected and wonderful happens: a new phrase takes wings, soaring freely above the words. By repeating the last line it gains space, growing into four bars, and this new phrase is of such magnificence as cannot be described or explained. It expresses all the joy, all the bliss a human heart can contain:

A form of expression brought to such unprecedented perfection —and the above example is no rarity but one of the blossoms that spring up everywhere from Schubert's fertile imagination— would be unthinkable if the creative act were not concentrated on the all-embracing phenomenon of melody. In this, his most personal secret is a gracefulness of contour which has rarely been equalled and never been surpassed by any other, a contour which, undulating with the most natural ease, always offers unusual perspectives. One has only to think of a tune which, for a hundred years, has been firmly anchored in the memory of everyone to whom music means anything, the second subject in the first movement of the Unfinished Symphony:

One does not realise how subtly this seemingly simple, easy-flowing melody is constructed; its first four bars, playing with the two little motifs a and b, follow the pattern a b b a. How unusual this is one only recognises when one tries to give this invention a conventional shape, such as a b a b:

It is hardly necessary to add that one may discover peculiarities every bit as subtle in the works of other great composers. The extraordinary thing with Schubert is that his melodies are so natural and self-evident as to give the impression that they must have existed since the creation of the world. The error of mistaking this naturalness for banality has been committed from the beginning, and it can already be found among Schubert's contemporary critics. When one year before his death his *Valses nobles* were published, the critic of the Leipzig *Allgemeine musikalische Zeitung* found it necessary to take the composer to task: "The critic cannot discover from these dances what the epithet '*nobles*' means. They are not bad, but no more than ordinary. . . ."

It contributed to the peculiar formation of Schubert's melodic idiom that it reached maturity during the early years when his work was mainly devoted to song-writing. Generally speaking, his thematic invention is predominantly determined by a type of melody pertaining to the song. With him one can rarely find an instrumental theme that is not eminently singable. This makes these inventions so wonderfully expressive, but on the other hand it makes their symphonic treatment extra-ordinarily difficult, a point which will be taken up later. A song tune is a finished product, complete in itself. It does not demand, nor does it readily submit to, thematic development, which is, however, the end and aim of symphonic style. The result is a contradiction in terms which Schubert, at the time of his maturity, was able to resolve, or rather to circumvent, in his own way.

What makes his melodies so blissful in their effect is their relaxed ease, again something diametrically opposed to the dynamic pregnancy of a symphonic motif. Schubert's melody opens up, expands and sings with inexhaustible breath; and, as we have seen in "Du bist die Ruh", when it already seems to be descending to its conclusion, it may rise again to a new climax of expressive beauty. In another case it is a postlude, as a rule hardly more than a formal rounding-off, where the invention soars to its most glorious expressiveness, as in "An die Musik", a song with which Schubert has unwittingly raised a lasting monument to his friend Schober, the author of the poem:

Melody was for Schubert the highest, most consummate achievement, and this can be seen at its clearest when he writes variations. It is here that the contrast between him and his contemporary Beethoven becomes most evident. For Beethoven the aim of variation is to transform the theme into a different entity, something new and unexpected. He himself liked to translate the term into German, using the word *Veränderungen* (transformations). He objectifies the theme, turning it into an impersonal framework, as it were, on which to build new and different inventions. And Brahms, who followed his lead when writing variations, preferred themes by other composers—Handel, Schumann, Haydn, Paganini—for the same reason: he could treat them with more detached objectivity. With Schubert, who liked to write variations on his own song tunes, the theme only becomes still more intense in its original expressiveness. Using the richer means afforded by instruments, it rises to a higher form of manifestation, a richer incarnation of its original character, which nevertheless remains essentially unchanged.

I am attempting here not an analysis of Schubert's works but a kind of morphology of his music, illustrated by typical examples. As far as variations are concerned, two works will offer sufficient insight into the peculiarities of his treatment of the form: the "Trout" Quintet, his earliest representative chamber music work, and the String Quartet in D minor ("Death and the Maiden"). In both works it is a middle movement in which a song tune is featured as a theme with variations. And in both cases the song concerned has given its imprint to the whole work, not in a thematic but in a poetic sense, as an emotional background. It would be ludicrous to think in terms of programme music in such a case: it is nothing of the kind, as there is no attempt whatever to depict anything extra-musical. Schubert, the lyricist, is infused with the expressive atmosphere of the poem he has set, and out of which his music has arisen; this intense feeling permeates the whole work; the poem has inspired it without any conscious intention on the part of the composer. More than any of the great masters Schubert was a tone poet, not deliberately or consciously, but purely out of the need of a poetically sensitive soul to express itself.

The "Trout" is a spring idyll, nature and everyday life observed by an idle onlooker in a state of contented well-being; a Phaeacian in the countryside; an easy-going, graceful melody; in all its simplicity and artlessness an immortal song. When from such a mood Schubert arrives at a large-scale instrumental creation, the landscape broadens and deepens and the richest, most sumptuous inventions take shape against this background of serene contemplation, only rarely crossed by a hint of something more serious and reflective. Three movements, drawing on the richest inspiration—allegro vivace, andante, scherzo—follow each other like different aspects of the same idyllic world. Then follow the variations on the song that has given the quintet its name and character, and this movement, interpolated before the finale, contains the quintessence of the whole work. As a theme for variations the tune has been slightly slowed down and rendered more simple and pensive by the omission of the lively, gracefully undulating motif of the accompaniment, as if the composer had at first confined himself to the background of the scene, the peaceful, green spring landscape. In the following variations the theme moves from one instrument to another without essentially changing its structure, but becoming ever richer in colour, the mood abandoning itself more and more to the beauty of the moment, until finally, in the last variation, the trout, with the original accompaniment of the song, starts its lively sport in the water. And thus this wonderful movement comes to an end, as if with a last look at the charming landscape; nothing is now needed except a cheerfully sauntering finale without a single cloud in the sky, a movement whose lightheartedness only a pedant could resent.

Just as the spring landscape underlies the Quintet, so death looms obsessively behind the String Quartet in D minor, as the inescapable background to all four movements. The contrast between these two works gives some impression of the breadth of imagination which characterises the range of Schubert's world. What is expressed in this quartet reaches far beyond the song and its words to the eternal question of the enigma and the inexorability of death. And just as the idea extends into the vast and epic, so the theme, borrowed from his song "Death and the Maiden", is not simply taken over as it stood, but is treated as free material, transformed and reshaped. It is as if a general, all-embracing conclusion had been drawn from a single tragic case.

As has already been stated, nothing could be more erroneous than to think of a programmatic intention. Schubert's music is emotionally inspired; he can only create out of an overflowing heart. If it was a song written seven years earlier that came to his mind at that time, he was driven to it by a compelling feeling that demanded expression. One can easily understand that the thought of death was uppermost in the mind of a man who had gone through a grave illness and must have been conscious of acute danger. From the tragic intensity of the first movement to the breathless dance of death of the finale the images only change within a narrow spectrum of dark hues. A line by Schiller could serve as a motto for the whole work:

> Auch das Schöne muss sterben, das Menschen und Götter bezwinget.
> ("And beauty too must die that conquers Gods and men.")

Even the scherzo reflects a desperate determination and a darkness, and the idyllic trio only seems to accentuate this through poignant contrast. The variations take the place of a slow movement. The theme, starting in a deeply serious, meditative mood, moves, without significantly changing its melodic substance, from one variation to another with gradually increasing rhythmic frequency and ever more passionate expressiveness to a dynamic climax from which it sinks steadily to quiet resignation. Here, as in the Quintet, the melody with its variations is the emotional nucleus of a work that has grown from a complex of feelings latent in the song from which it came.

It was inevitable that the *lied* should have been at the centre of this discussion of Schubert's melody. From wherever one tries to approach the topic, one will be led back to the *lied*, and it is from there that we shall have to explore the problems of Schubert's world, his individuality and his development.

3

THE ERUPTION OF THE LIED

THE EVENT IS extraordinary, indeed well-nigh unique. As a rule, artistic developments proceed in an organic way, not always without impediments, but nevertheless in an ascending curve and with a steadily growing realisation of the aim. The *lied* which Schubert created and which, as a supreme achievement, has remained exemplary, appeared like an eruption in a first, magnificent masterpiece. No visible path leads towards it; the works of others before him have as little direct relationship to it as have his own previous attempts in which just occasionally, as in a sudden spark, the light which guides him becomes apparent. And this miraculous single achievement is still far from signifying a breakthrough. There are numerous relapses until, after years of toil and trouble, the results match the intention and consummate mastery has been attained. Only a couple of months before this first prodigious work of genius, "Gretchen am Spinnrade", Schubert, with a setting of Schiller's ballad "Der Taucher", had created a veritable monster, a piece of incredible bombast, thirty pages long. A setting of another ballad by Schiller, "Die Bürgschaft", written in the same style one year later, shows little progress. Yet not long afterwards, with achievements such as "Erlkönig", "An Schwager Kronos", and "Der Wanderer", the goal seems to be almost definitively reached, the way assured to the perfect realisation of a lyrical work of art in which every expressive detail of the words is followed and yet the whole has an impeccable formal unity—Schubert's own unique vision of the *lied*.

He wrote his first song at the age of fourteen. It has not been established how he came to embark upon this musical sidetrack, lying as it did outside the sphere in which he moved at the Court Chapel and in his school. He had sung all his life. A bright child with real enthusiasm for music takes an interest in everything musical which comes his way. Undoubtedly his interest was furthered by a natural instinct, by the emotion a line of poetry and its expressive translation into a musical phrase evoked in him. But, as already mentioned, his teacher Salieri was not sparing in his disgruntled remarks about the uselessness of such a pursuit. He was, of course, an Italian and used to excuse his deficient knowledge of German with the remark that he had after all only lived in Vienna for fifty years. German poetry was a closed book to him. Young Schubert, notwithstanding his respect for his teacher, no doubt took account of this circumstance and did not allow himself to be discouraged.

The first question is: how did his inclination develop further? Here it becomes necessary to consider the state of the German song at the time when Schubert made his first attempts of this kind. There have always been songs, both spiritual and secular. The songs by Haydn, Mozart and Beethoven offer enough material for examining the nature and the limitations of the genre at the highest level attained at that time. One thing has to be stated at once: for none of these three great masters was the song more than an occasionally cultivated trifle, though Beethoven did at times give it more serious attention. But it was too remote a subject for him and during the last ten years of his life, except for some occasional compositions, he hardly ever thought of writing songs. For Mozart and Haydn the song was a small form, belonging in the same category as the arietta in an opera, and it did not occur to either of them to pay more attention to the words than in the case of an operatic aria, where, even if the text was determined by the dramatic situation, the words themselves were treated more or less as raw material and not as the very centre of the artistic problem. It is different with Beethoven who, belonging to a new generation, was a sincere admirer of Goethe and certainly had a genuine feeling for poetry. He set a number of Goethe poems to music, one of them, "Nur wer die Sehnsucht kennt", four times, but without ever touching more than the surface of their emotional content. That a young beginner should find what he, the giant of all giants, had sought in vain, gives us an idea of Schubert's immense achievement, but it also shows what specific faculties were required to solve such a specific problem. Even a genius has his limitations, just as he has his own special gifts. Beethoven never felt completely at home with vocal composition, in spite of the greatness of *Fidelio*, the *Missa Solemnis* and the Choral Symphony, whereas vocal expression was, as it were, Schubert's artistic mother tongue; this may to some extent explain the difficulties of the one, the triumph of the other.

But this is not to disparage Beethoven's vocal masterpieces; in this field too he was a giant. When his deepest feelings are aroused, as in the works mentioned, he rises to his greatest heights, and even in his songs his personality is unmistakable. But here he does not seem to be aiming sufficiently high. Nowhere does he exceed the middle region of his expressive gamut.

The song, or—to give it its proper name—the arietta, as it is found in Haydn and perhaps even more typically in Mozart, is a product of rococo style. The pastoral prettiness of Goethe's operettas, or *Singspiele* as they were called, (*Die Laune des Verliebten*, *Jery und Bätely* and *Erwin und Elmire*, all written for the Weimar court) is the most accomplished artistic expression of this courtly, aristocratic fashion. The words of Mozart's most famous song, "Das Veilchen", stem from the last-named of these divertissements and could fittingly be sung there in the appropriate costume. It is indicative of Mozart's attitude towards the text he used that he added to the poem a little appendix which came straight from his heart, but which must have sent a shiver down Goethe's spine because, to use Schiller's term, it makes his poem "sentimental":

> Das arme Veilchen!
> Es war ein herzigs Veilchen.
>
> (Poor violet!
> It was a dear little violet.)

With all its genuinely Mozartian charm, even this little gem remains tied to the stylised world of the rococo. Mozart created living, breathing human beings in his operas. In "Das Veilchen" a doll acts in the garb of a shepherdess.

The eighteenth-century song is predominantly strophic; thus the problem of form is solved in the simplest way, and subject

matter and expression are confined to the conventional sentimentality of German poetry before Lessing. A delightful
definition of a song can be found in the *Dictionary of Music*
of 1767 by Jean-Jacques Rousseau, the philosopher and
musician:

> Chanson: Espèce de petit poème lyrique fort court, qui roule
> ordinairement sur des sujets agréables, auquel on ajoute un
> air pour être chanté dans des occasions familières, comme
> à table, avec ses amis, avec sa maitresse, et même seul,
> pour éloigner quelques instants l'ennui si l'on est riche, et
> pour supporter plus doucement la misère et le travail si l'on
> est pauvre.
>
> (Song: a type of short lyrical poem, usually on a pleasant
> topic, to which a tune is added, to be sung at homely occasions
> such as at table, with one's friends, with one's mistress, or
> even alone, to while away some moments of boredom if one
> is rich, or to alleviate one's misery and fatigue if one is poor.)

The limitations in the range of expression thus indicated
still hold true for most of Beethoven's songs. With one of them,
however, he almost broke new ground—but not quite, because
the range of feeling is too narrow to give richer content to the
new form he has created. It is the cycle *An die ferne Geliebte*
(To the Distant Beloved), which, starting with a strophic
melody, repeated five times, moves in a wide arc through
changing episodes, and leads back to the original melody
followed by a lively, effective coda. Schubert, too, set mediocre
poetry to music; but this *Liederkreis* (song-cycle) by Beethoven,
the first ever written, suffers from an intolerable type of
doggerel verse for which it is impossible to find a good
word.

Alois Jeitteles, the author of these sentimental rhymes, seems
to have enjoyed some reputation at the time. What Beethoven
made of these verses shows character and sensitivity. The
master's hand reveals itself in the fine invention and the clearly
sculptured form. But nowhere does the emotional intensity
rise above a certain middle level, and thus in the end the whole
cycle remains within the confines of the pastoral idyll of the
eighteenth century. Incidentally, this work was written two
years later than Schubert's first epoch-making *lied*-creations,

of which, however, Beethoven could have had no knowledge.

Naturally, at this time, as at every other, there was no lack of pygmies, those would-be composers who always tend to fill the foreground and who in due course disappear. Johann Friedrich Reichardt (1752–1814) and Carl Friedrich Zelter (1758–1832), both friends of Goethe, whose poems they set to music, were popular song-writers and young Schubert must have known their works. Their music has been justly forgotten. Another esteemed contemporary, Johann Rudolf Zumsteeg (1760–1802), left visible traces in Schubert's music and these are worth following up, not because of this composer's intrinsic merit, which was negligible, but because this will give some idea of the distance Schubert had to cover. His first song, "Hagars Klage" ("Hagar's Lament"), which, as already mentioned, he wrote at the age of fourteen, follows Zumsteeg's setting of the same poem with the ingenuous innocence of a schoolboy. Mandyczewski, the editor of the *lied* section in the Complete Edition of Schubert's Works, added this and two other ballads by Zumsteeg, "Die Erwartung" and "Ritter Toggenburg", as an appendix because they show a close affinity to Schubert's settings of the same Schiller poems. In this connection it is worth mentioning that at Schubert's time and even long afterwards a simple and obvious method was employed in teaching composition: the student had to reproduce faithfully, both in form and character, what was considered to be an exemplary model. It can be demonstrated by other examples, too, that Schubert was familiar with this method and made use of it. The amazing thing is that "Die Erwartung" was written four years later, "Ritter Toggenburg" even five, than that first-born, "Hagars Klage", and yet in "Toggenburg" Schubert still follows Zumsteeg's model in every detail of the lay-out, stumbling with him through episodes of recitativo and aria, and ending like him with five strophic repetitions when, in the last five stanzas of Schiller's poem, the action becomes static. No exercise could have been carried out with more modesty and fidelity. One can see how long and arduous Schubert's self-taught apprenticeship was, and with what perseverance he "exercised his pen". For "Toggenburg" is still hardly more than an exercise, even if the style has become more assured and mature.

The initial attractions for Schubert in Zumsteeg's ballads were the richer possibilities of "through-composed" form, a larger type of composition, based upon a more circumstantial lay-out. By freely changing the treatment of the various stanzas of a poem, by alternating recitativo and arioso, by changing key, time, and speed, Zumsteeg tries to do justice to the changing content and mood of the poem, and this evidently suited Schubert's feeling better than the old strophic form of the eighteenth-century ballad, where a sufficiently objective and simple melody, repeated any number of times, as required, had to fit any change of mood, and where it was the singer's job to supply the necessary flexibility of expression. In his through-composed ballads Zumsteeg is noticeably influenced by the operatic style of his period. His only virtue is careful declamation and this quality seems to have appealed to Schubert, for it occasionally happens that he even copies one of Zumsteeg's phrases practically note for note. The way in which Zumsteeg constructs his ballads would still be objectionable, even if his invention were less thin and conventional. Yet Schubert persistently follows him. He fumbles in the undefined realm between words and music, trips up a great deal, loses himself in bombast, becomes entangled in a thicket, and is unable to find his way back to the main key. A labyrinth without Ariadne's thread! Here and there he succeeds in creating an imaginative episode, but, with such an impossible formal design, he has just as little chance of arriving at a satisfactory solution as his model ever had.

Thus one can see why Zumsteeg has, both rightly and wrongly, been regarded as Schubert's forerunner: rightly, because, stimulated by him, he persistently followed Zumsteeg's path for a number of years; and wrongly, because it was a wrong track leading him into the undergrowth, and a forerunner in the proper sense can really only be one who has found the right path, even though he may not have reached the goal. To arrive at the true *lied*, Schubert had to overcome Zumsteeg's pseudo-form as well as the primitive strophic song, the two premises from which he started. Only with a comprehensive view of the whole development can one obtain an idea of his character, his single-mindedness and his alert artistic instinct. To call this somnambulism is to give the term a wrong meaning.

What Schubert achieved, at first in individual instances and ultimately as the result of purposeful application of his artistic awareness, was the momentous innovation of an art-form in which poetry and music are fused into something richer, deeper, and more moving than had ever been accomplished by the two sister-arts, singly or in conjunction.

It is clear that such a result could not have involved the musician alone. If one examines the songs of Schubert's apprenticeship, with all their weaknesses and gradual improvements, and realises how even in an insignificant poem a deeper thought or graceful image could fire the composer's imagination, while, on the other hand, he had to struggle, with all the skill he had acquired, to overcome flat, prosaic passages, and still failed to succeed, one can only conclude, though one should have known it at the outset, that a composer of Schubert's poetic sensitivity depends for better or for worse on the poem he sets to music. If one also looks at the great achievements of this period of development, works which tower above their environment like mountain peaks, one cannot but recognise that all roads lead in one direction, to a single focal point: Goethe.

Here is the key to the miracle, to that burst of creative genius in Schubert's first master-song, "Gretchen am Spinnrade". The spark which set off the explosion was his first full contact with the fountainhead of poetic inspiration. As if the semi-darkness in which he had been groping for years had suddenly been illuminated by a radiant light, he now saw the solution before him, within his reach. Psychiatrists speak of the "trauma", the fatal experience which does lasting harm to a psyche. If this exists, then presumably there must also be an experience that, like a flash of lightning, ignites a receptive mind and makes it productive. "*Incipit vita nova*": thus Dante has sung of it.

What the young assistant schoolmaster experienced at that moment borders on the inconceivable. There is only one answer to the naïve question "How could a seventeen-year-old grasp with such depth the states and ecstasies of a woman's soul?": the poet's words awakened his heart and his power of imagination. Through the magic of Goethe's poem Gretchen became for him a more direct experience than anything he had encountered in reality. And Goethe remained—this is a main argument for this interpretation—the most abundant source of inspiration for the songs Schubert wrote during the following years, as is unmistakable in such summits as "Nähe des Geliebten", "Rastlose Liebe", "Heidenröslein", "An Schwager Kronos", and "Erlkönig". For the creation of Schubert's *lied* two equally rare qualities, developed to the fullest, had to be combined: an unlimited wealth of melodic invention, and the most spontaneous feeling for the emotion and expression contained in a poet's words. Schubert's unique gift of poetic receptivity apparently needed a decisive impulse in order to become creative in the highest sense. He received this impulse through the encounter with Goethe's lyrical poetry.

Never has there been anything more providential than this uniting of two minds in a work of art. And at this point it is necessary to go further back into the past in order to explain why poetry and music were ready at that very moment in history to achieve an unprecedented fusion and fulfilment. The reader's forgiveness is asked for a short historical digression; it seems unavoidable since its subject, the relationship of poetry and music, has to the best of my knowledge hardly ever been treated comprehensively.

At an archaic stage of all known cultural developments the poem was sung; poetry and music were inseparably combined. In Greek, the word *musiké* (from which "music" is derived) means both poetry and music, the arts of the muses. This close relationship persisted during the early Middle Ages: not only in Gregorian chant, the liturgical music of the early Church, which had its roots in antiquity, but even when, in the thirteenth century, the lyrical art of the Troubadours and the *Minnesänger* was in full flower. At that time, however, the beginnings of polyphony had already turned the evolution of music in a completely different direction, one which was to become decisive for its whole modern development. The price to be paid for this was a temporary estrangement from the sister art, for the enormous structural problems which had to be solved would not tolerate a dependent role. Music far outgrew its poetic material, and even in sacred music the matching of the text was largely left to chance. This was one of the reasons why at the Council of Trent (1545–63) serious attempts were made to ban polyphonic music from the Church altogether, and to revert to Gregorian chant. The attempt failed, most of all because a more word-conscious treatment of vocal music was already under way; and, in the course of the century, this led to the fullest artistic perfection with Palestrina, Victoria, Lassus, and the Italian and English madrigalists.

This development, however, was again superseded by a far more radical one, the reduction of the vocal line to recitativo in the earliest Florentine and Venetian experiments with opera, which were inspired by a true Renaissance idea, the attempt to recreate the supposed style of ancient drama. Yet one main result of the conquest of polyphony could not be eliminated by the *stile recitativo*, whose chief aim was perfect clarity of the words: harmony. This remained when counterpoint was temporarily ousted. It was no longer possible to return to the single vocal line of antiquity or of Gregorian chant. And polyphony, first banned by the "moderns" of the early seventeenth century, slipped in, as it were, by the backdoor, in the *stile concertato*. So there were now two, three, or even four competing parts forming the main texture above a harmonic accompaniment, and with this technique instrumental style energetically took the lead. The earliest attempts at independent instrumental music in the sixteenth century had followed the formal structure of vocal music. In the course of the seventeenth century the process was reversed: vocal music followed the various formal patterns of the now vigorously progressing instrumental writing.

Over the transition period towers the mighty figure of Heinrich Schütz (1585–1672), a German trained in Italy, who reconciled the inherited polyphonic vocal style with the recitativo of modern monody, and arrived at a combination of melody, shaped with great form-consciousness, and expressive declamation, in a style of writing whose structural potential went far beyond the narrow limits of recitativo. Here we are for the first time confronted with a great musician for whom the words are as important as their translation into a perfectly shaped melodic phrase. And the word is the word of God, Luther's translation of the Bible, the first magnificent codification of modern German, and Schütz's lifelong inspiration.

It is unlikely that Schubert ever even heard the name of

Schütz. But developments move in spirals. Schütz was the first to create a genuinely articulated vocal style in German music, as Schubert did, two centuries later, by totally different means. As the creator of a German vocal style Schütz was in fact his most distinguished forerunner, though at a stage of musical development which confined a vocal structure to the narrowest formal dimensions.[1] It is, to put it plainly, music before the discovery of more highly organised formal principles. The extended, solidly constructed form into which such an invention could have grown had yet to be created, and this was a task too great for vocal music with its organic limitations. The musician's instinct for form, driving him beyond such narrow confines, again broke that fusion of words and music which had been achieved for a brief historical moment. Music was too self-willed, too strongly impelled by its own creative urge, to be subdued for long by the word. Schütz was forgotten, as was Monteverdi in Italy, and, in England, the extraordinary word-consciousness of the Elizabethan madrigal and lute song and of Purcell's vocal style. The instrumental composer, who took the lead in the development of form in the seventeenth century, paid little attention to the expressive fusion of words and music: this was relegated to recitativo.

These remarks are not contradicted by the fact that it was just at this period that Italian *bel canto* celebrated its first triumphs. The style of Italian baroque opera is based on a vocal technique whose most characteristic element, coloratura, is as completely unfettered by words as an instrument. The words, repeated as often as required—an aria rarely has more than four lines of text—can be replaced by others without difficulty, and the composer often takes advantage of this by re-using an aria in another work, with different words. The majority of the arias and choruses in Bach's *Christmas Oratorio* are, to use the technical term, "parodies"; they are taken, with the words changed, from various secular cantatas. Handel very frequently adopted the same procedure. In these circumstances it is understandable that the poet of an opera or an oratorio became a mere librettist, and text-writing a humble craft. In his arias Bach is always inspired by a poetic idea that

[1] After writing this, I have found valuable remarks on Schütz in *Schubert, Musik und Lyrik* by Thrasybulos Georgiades (Göttingen, 1967).

stimulates his imagination. But he treats the prosody of the words with the greatest unconcern, and the less attention one pays to these ungainly verses, which stem from the worst period of decay in German poetry, the early eighteenth century, the better. In coloratura the music outgrows the words, following its natural instinct for form. The word is not a vehicle of expression but simply raw material for the music.

This is not meant as an aesthetic disparagement; in the hands of a master—such as Handel, Bach, Pergolesi, or Mozart—this style finds its full justification. But what can be seen here is a complete separation of music and poetry, if one takes the latter term in its highest sense. Baroque music has nothing to do with poetry, however poetic the composer may be in his musical expression.

Gluck, in the second half of the eighteenth century, was probably the first great musician to have a feeling for such subtleties, though admittedly far more with respect to dramatic structure than to the text of his librettos; and as these were Italian or French, he probably faced the problem of German declamation for the first time when, in his old age, he set Klopstock's odes to music. And Mozart, though he had an infallible feeling for the stage, had, like his predecessors, grown up with the conventions of Italian opera. Da Ponte was a skilful dramatist and Schikaneder a stalwart of the theatre, but without Mozart none of their verse would ever have had a chance of surviving for posterity. Mozart had neither the time, the possibility, nor the critical judgment, to search for something that did not exist: a true poet who would write a libretto for him. He had long been dead when Goethe had the odd idea of writing a second part of *The Magic Flute*, something which remained a fragment. Mozart's composition of "Das Veilchen" was an instinctive act of genius which remained an isolated occurrence, his only encounter with great poetry. And Beethoven, who had a more direct feeling for literature and who revered Goethe, swallowed without demur what the questionable librettist of *Fidelio* put before him. When, in one of the most sublime moments of deep emotion in the quartet "Mir ist so wunderbar", poor Jacquino sings "Mir sträubt sich schon das Haar, der Vater willigt ein" ("My hair does stand on end, the father will consent"), there is nothing one can do but acknowledge that even Beethoven, as an operatic composer, could tolerantly accept verse that makes one shudder.

But that poetry and music were ready to join hands again just at this time was due to the state of development of the two arts, which had apparently been estranged for centuries. German poetry of the baroque period, like its music, is enclosed in an artificial but in its own way attractive formal pattern, often overburdened with conceptual and mythological conceits which were to persist far into the eighteenth century. The poet spoke from a pedestal from which Goethe, with the magnificent simplicity and directness of his lyrical poetry, was the first to descend. His verse, as remote from baroque bombast as from rococo affectation, called for a new mode of musical treatment. And music, which in its own way had progressed to a simpler, less involved structure, culminating in the ideal classical balance of form and expression, was now able to solve a problem to which the preceding generation would not have been equal. It may perhaps be that this task also required a musician like Schubert, who was naïve and unsophisticated enough not to be inhibited by a venerable heritage, a musician capable of meeting something as elemental as Goethe's lyrical poetry with a correspondingly elemental, completely unspoiled receptivity. Music, now in sovereign control of its fully expanded technical and structural means, could with Schubert find its way back to its most natural and most direct form of utterance: melody.

From the unique constellation which brought together Schubert's music and Goethe's poetry, the *lied* was born. The vitality and fecundity of this new species has been proved by its capacity for development. The *lieder* of Schumann, Brahms and Wolf would have been unthinkable without Schubert's example. And the novelty and peculiarity of this art-form is demonstrated by the fact that, both in French and in English, the term *lied* has been adopted. It would not have done to call it *chanson* or *song*.

The fact that in the first quarter of the nineteenth century a German of almost the same age as Schubert was able to arrive at a similarly fruitful synthesis, quite independently and without any knowledge of Schubert's work, seems to confirm that the time had come to achieve a genuine coalescence of words and music. Carl Loewe was certainly not one of the great. His actual songs, to say nothing of his dust-covered oratorios, operas and string quartets, hardly stand out from the average second-rate music of his time. But he found a genuine, excellently balanced form for the ballad, and among the three hundred or more pieces of this kind which he wrote—he set any ballad he could lay his hands on—at least a dozen have stood the test of time just as well as any minor masterpiece could. His manner of composition, like Schubert's, originated in a vivid feeling for declamation and expression, and his remarkable talent for form enabled him, by combining repetition and contrast, to achieve a clearly defined structure akin to an instrumental rondo, thus solving the very serious problem posed for the composer by a long poem with many stanzas. Loewe's setting of "Erlkönig", written not much later than Schubert's which, of course, was unknown at that time, has been overshadowed by the latter. Otherwise it would be one of the best existing compositions of its kind. Loewe's device of individualising the voice of the Erlkönig by giving him a striking, recurrent motif, always in the same key—incidentally an amazing premonition of Wagner's Rhinegold-motif—is uncannily effective, however limited his melodic invention appears when compared with Schubert's. And with "Prinz Eugen", where, with gripping effect, he used one of the most characteristic of old German folksongs, he created something as immortal as an otherwise very mortal man ever could.

How far philosophical insight and reasoning can fail to keep pace with the artist's instinctive vision is demonstrated by the fact that the keenest, most comprehensive intellect of the period, Schopenhauer, who was, however, almost as ignorant of the music of his time as Goethe, did not have the faintest notion that such an ideal union of the two sister arts could be possible. His words on this subject, written after Schubert's death, correspond roughly to the aesthetic conditions of vocal music in the eighteenth century:

As surely as music, far from being ancillary to poetry, is an independent art, nay, the mightiest of all, and achieves all its ends by its own means, just as surely music is not dependent on the words that are sung. . . . The words are, and remain, a foreign addition to music, of subordinate value, because the impression of the sound is much more powerful, inescapable and rapid than that of the words. These, when incorporated into music, can therefore only have a subordinate function and must accordingly accommodate themselves to it.

Goethe has often been bitterly blamed for ignoring the young musician who turned so many of his poems into immortal songs. On the other hand, no one as yet seems to have assessed the full extent of Schubert's debt to the poet. Admittedly, the case is complicated enough to explain misjudgments. It is a fact that in April 1816 a book, containing sixteen Schubert settings of Goethe's poems, including "Erlkönig", "Rastlose Liebe", "Gretchen am Spinnrade", and "Heidenröslein", was sent to Goethe in a neatly handwritten copy; they were not yet published. This package was accompanied by a letter of recommendation from Schubert's friend Josef von Spaun. It was not acknowledged, and the book was later returned to the sender without comment.

One cannot read of this without distress—to be rebuffed was Schubert's everlasting destiny, but this was perhaps the worst and most humiliating incident. Even so, this does not justify moral condemnation of the poet, who committed this sin through his fateful ignorance. He was old and tired. Consignments of this kind, recommendations, humble applications, poured in daily. Here was music by an unknown young composer, one among so many. And Spaun's formal, stilted letter, tinged with the Austrian civil service style—it is printed in O. E. Deutsch's Documentary Biography of Schubert—was hardly such as to arouse Goethe's sympathy. His ability to read music was poor, and at Weimar he rarely had a musician at hand who could have instructed him. It is quite conceivable that the consignment was laid aside without further examination.

This explanation, though perhaps correct, is not fully convincing; for, nine years later, in June 1825, Schubert himself sent Goethe his three recently published songs Op. 19 ("An Schwager Kronos", "An Mignon", "Ganymed"), "Dedicated to the poet in veneration", with the following accompanying letter:

Your Excellency,

If by the dedication of this setting of your poems I could succeed in recording my unlimited veneration of Your Excellency, and perhaps in gaining some attention for my humble self, I would praise the favourable outcome of this wish as the happiest event of my life.

    With the greatest respect,
      Your most devoted servant,
        Franz Schubert

Goethe noted the receipt of this package in his diary; but he left it unacknowledged, just as in the first case, and this circumstance makes one suspect that there was more behind it than mere lack of interest. First of all, one must take into consideration the generation gap, which is particularly accentuated by the fact that the poet, having grown up with the strophic song of the mid-eighteenth century, was never willing to accept any other musical treatment of his poems, as is attested by his recorded utterances. His friends Reichardt and Zelter, who set many of his poems to music, may have confirmed him in this view because it was their own. Furthermore, it must be taken into account that Goethe, who was as closely familiar with all branches of the visual arts as he was with poetry, had no similarly intimate knowledge of music. In Weimar there was little musical stimulation. The young Mendelssohn's letter to his parents about a visit he paid to the eighty-year-old poet shows an ignorance of music on Goethe's part which can only be attributed to an almost provincial isolation:

> . . . Goethe is so friendly and affectionate with me that I do not know how to thank him or how to deserve it. In the morning I must play the piano for him for about an hour, pieces by all the great composers, in chronological order, and tell him what new developments they brought about; meanwhile he sits in a dark corner like *Jupiter tonans*, with his old eyes flashing. He would have none of Beethoven. But I told him I could not help that, and thereupon played him the first movement of the Symphony in C minor. This affected him strangely. At first he said "but it does not move one at all; it merely astounds; it is grandiose", and went on growling to himself, until after a long time he began again:

"That is very great, quite mad, one is almost afraid the house will collapse; and imagine when they are all playing this together!" And at table, in the middle of something else, he again began to talk about it. . . .

The work with which Goethe was confronted for the first time on that occasion was Beethoven's Fifth Symphony, which for two decades had been in the repertoire of every orchestra in Europe. It is understandable that to a man who was so out of touch with music something as unfamiliar as Schubert's great lyrical creations, reaching far beyond the scope of anything that had been known hitherto, would appear merely frightening. And most of all they must have seemed totally foreign to his own conception of his poems. It would be asking too much to expect him to have recognised immediately that he had before him a new art-form. Even his prejudice in favour of the strophic song cannot be held against a poet with Goethe's sensitive feeling for form, as this was for him the only possible way of completely preserving the integrity of his poem. Anything beyond a clear, pleasant melodic treatment of his verse, leaving the appropriate expression and emphasis to the singer, he found unnecessary, even harmful. If, as is very probable, his ability to read music failed him in the face of Schubert's compositions, one thing he must have seen: that the composer had taken liberties with the poem; and this hurt his feelings. Just as every note matters to the composer, so every syllable of the verse structure is rightly essential to the poet, and hence even the repetition of words may annoy him because it distorts the original form. Even the wonderfully moving effect of repeating the first line, "Meine Ruh ist hin, mein Herz ist schwer" ("My peace is gone, my heart is sore") at the end of "Gretchen am Spinnrade" may have been lost on the poet, who could only see in it a violation of his original concept.

This, however, is a superficial detail of a state of affairs whose essence has much deeper roots. Goethe's Gretchen is a child of the people. Her language, her whole way of thinking and expression, is based upon this characteristic; a song sung by such a girl would naturally be a folksong. This holds true of her monologue at the spinning-wheel, as it does of another of her songs, "Der König in Thule", which, incidentally, Schubert

composed two years later as a simple strophic song. The depth
of feeling, the passion and tragic intensity of "Gretchen am
Spinnrade", were so compelling for the composer that he had
to forget such limitations. The enormous gain thus achieved
was beyond the grasp of the poet, lacking as he did any sense for
this musical idiom. He may have noticed nothing but that his
poem had been flooded by foreign matter, that his Gretchen
was expressing herself in a musical language which contradicted his own idea of her. Her picture, as he saw it, had fallen
out of its dramatic frame.

Can the extent of this tragedy ever be assessed: two contemporaries passing each other by, while their spiritual ties,
heightened to their fullest potential, stand there in a unique
art-form? Schubert must have realised it. It was his fate to be
rejected, and such repeated experiences must have had a
cumulative effect. A kind word could have comforted him.
It was not the first time that the Olympian had caused grievous
psychological harm to a defenceless victim; young Hölderin
may have been a similar case.

Goethe in his majestic isolation could not have had the
slightest inkling of it. Even less could he have anticipated what
an inspiration music, which meant so little to him, would draw
from his work for the next hundred years—more than from
any other poet before or after him. Think, apart from Schubert
and Beethoven (*Egmont*), of Mendelssohn (*Walpurgisnacht*),
Schumann (*Scenes from Faust*), Berlioz (*The Damnation of Faust*),
Liszt (*Faust Symphony*), Wagner (*Faust Overture*), Brahms
(*Rinaldo, Alto Rhapsody, Song of Destiny*), Wolf (*Fifty Goethe
Songs*), Mahler (Eighth Symphony), not to mention all the
"Faust" operas. It looks as if musicians, whose creative experience is rooted in a more emotional sphere, showed a better
understanding of the mighty stature of Goethe than the poets
of the following generation, who, torn between embarrassed
respect, mistrust and hidden dislike, betray very mixed feelings.
It remains Schubert's merit to have welded together music
and poetry on the highest level of expressiveness. Who was the
donor, who the recipient, is immaterial. The decisive fact
remains that from the conjunction of these two creative powers
there grew one of the most magnificent artistic flowers of all
time.

4

PROBLEMS AND SOLUTIONS

S CHUBERT'S ERRATIC DEVELOPMENT, with its alternation
of flashes of genius, mediocrity, and total failure, is typical of
an artist whose creative urge is stronger than his critical control,
and who is, in all essentials, left to his own devices, without
example or guidance. Experience was his only school. Through
untiring efforts he developed his own technique which,
together with his miraculous sensitivity, enabled him to do
justice to the form and character of any poetic subject.

It is evident that, from a purely formal point of view, a strophic
poem invites a strophic setting. One must not assume that just
because Schubert had progressed beyond this form into a field
of unlimited possibilities, strophic song ceased to be of fundamental importance for him. Whenever he rejected it, he had
compelling reasons for doing so. But he came back to it over
and over again, and a glance at *Die schöne Müllerin* or *Winterreise*
will show how extraordinarily mature and expressive this
archetypal song-form, which had temporarily receded into the
background, had again become in Schubert's later works.

To start with the primary fact: any strophic poem can be
given a strophic setting if the composer treats the words in a
neutral, non-committal way, so to speak, scanning them rather
than reciting them. Consider a well-known example, Papageno's first song in Mozart's *Magic Flute*, where the popular
style of the tune avoids all problems of declamation in the
simplest way:

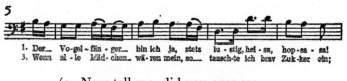

    (1. Now tell me, did you ever see
      So queer a kind of man as me?
    3. But there's a sport that's finer yet
      Than traps for silly birds to set.)

Slight lapses of declamation in the third stanza—wrong stresses in the second and third bars, which the translator, Edward Dent, has rightly eliminated in his English version—pose no problem for an experienced singer. As already explained, Mozart, whose literary education was scanty, never regarded the words as more than a catalyst for the music. He would never permit them to take control, an attitude which belonged to the style of his century. "In an opera poetry has to be the music's obedient daughter", he once wrote to his father. This is equally true for Bach, when he sets words to music, as, for instance, in the final chorus of the *St Matthew Passion,* where a deeply inspired melody distracts us from noticing that from the prosodic point of view it hardly fits the words:

("Here at Thy grave sit we all weeping.")

There are, of course, exceptions. Anyone who knows Bach's *Kreuzstab* Cantata ("Ich will den Kreuzstab gerne tragen"— "Gladly the cross I'd bear") will remember a wonderful phrase, brimming over with emotion, and matching the words to which it is composed with incomparable expressiveness and ideal articulation:

> Da leg ich den Kummer auf einmal ins Grab,
> Da wischt mir die Tränen mein Heiland selbst ab.

> (There will I entomb all my sorrow and sighs,
> My Saviour will wipe all the tears from my eyes.)[1]

The words bear the stamp of the sentimental pietism of the age. But they made Bach a tone poet because he was so deeply moved by them. He was clearly conscious of the extraordinary quality of his invention since, contrary to both the tradition of his time and his own custom, he reintroduced this phrase in the final recitativo of the cantata, like a reminiscence, a kind of

[1] Translations by Henry S. Drinker.

leit-motif. It is one of the inexplicable things about Bach, towering as he does over the centuries, that there is hardly any facet of form or expression in the music that came after him that he did not anticipate in his own way.

What appears here as a unique instance of expressiveness, reaching into the highest sphere of the transcendental, was with Schubert innate: the plastic modelling of a phrase out of the words, the deep feeling for the beauty of resonant syllables. This feeling led him to the song, and here he inevitably arrived at the limits of strophic possibilities, because even with an apparently regular metre accents often vary when the words are pressed into the far stricter form of the musical bar. In "Heidenröslein"—written when he was eighteen—the words fit the strophically repeated tune with perfect smoothness. He may not have taken any longer over this invention than the time he needed to write it down. But such precious gifts are rare, even with Schubert. Another strophic Goethe setting, "Nähe des Geliebten", dating from the same year, is an even maturer, and more magnificent product of a blessed hour:

The opening phrase, "Ich denke dein" ("I think of thee"), is, strictly speaking, commonplace, though it expands into a wonderfully noble melody. If it is sung with the simple, tender expression it demands, one has the impression that there has never been anything more beautiful or more blissful. This is the result of a perfect fusion of words and melody, the great secret that young Schubert discovered for himself. This simple phrase has the same magical effect when it returns in the second and third stanzas to the words "Ich sehe dich" ("I see you there") and "Ich höre dich" ("I hear your voice"). But anyone who has a feeling for such matters will be disappointed by this phrase in the last stanza. Here the words are "Ich bin bei dir" ("I am with you"), and the false accent on "bin" ("am") can hardly be camouflaged; the spell is broken.

Here lies the heart of the problem: How does the composer do justice to the prosodic vagaries so often contained in a great, profound poem? As already mentioned, this question can best be studied by comparing the different settings of the same poem that Schubert wrote when he was dissatisfied with the first version. Sometimes the new version dates from the following day, sometimes there are even three different settings, and such cases are a mine of information. There are three compositions of one of the Harpist's Songs from Goethe's *Wilhelm Meister*, "Wer nie sein Brot mit Tränen ass" ("Who never ate his bread in tears"), all written in September 1816, when Schubert was nineteen. A comparison of these provides a precious insight into Schubert's individual manner of composition, which was fundamentally different from Beethoven's scrupulous method of carefully working out every detail in his sketches, the method we know so well from the many sketches that have survived. It is quite plausible that Schubert's habit of writing down a composition at one sitting, with only rare corrections, was a result of the dreadful haste in which he was forced to work during the years of his development. First as a schoolboy, then for some years as a young schoolteacher, he was never master of his time. He could not afford the luxury of giving an invention time to mature. He wrote it down quickly in the form in which his imagination first conceived it. All too often disillusionment followed, a feeling of failure, and then he probably often found that it was not worth while improving and polishing. He put the unsatisfactory piece away in his drawer and tried a new setting, usually changing the time in order to change the whole direction of his invention. In the case mentioned above, the Harpist's Song, the second version was likewise discarded, and it was only a third one, published a number of years later, which satisfied his critical conscience.

> Wer nie sein Brot mit Tränen ass,
> Wer nie die kummervollen Nächte
> Auf seinem Bette weinend sass,
> Der kennt euch nicht, ihr himmlischen Mächte!

Ihr führt ins Leben uns hinein,
Ihr lasst den Armen schuldig werden,
Dann überlasst ihr ihn der Pein,
Denn alle Schuld rächt sich auf Erden.

(Who never ate his bread in tears,
Who has not spent the weary hours
In weeping till the dawn appears
He knows you not, o heavenly powers!

You made us frail and weak at birth,
You leave the guilty poor to languish;
Yet ev'ry wrong we do on earth
Will bring us care, torment and anguish.)[1]

At first sight there does not appear to be any difference in the verse structure of the two stanzas, and their emotional content does not seem to differ much either. This was also the composer's impression when he first set the song in strophic form:

etc.

But when he examined his composition critically, he was obviously put off by some wrong stresses in the second stanza, such as "Ihr führt ins Leben uns hinein" in the first two bars. And with growing awareness of the depth of the poem, he felt a heightening of intensity in the second stanza, with its tortured accusation and despair. So in a new composition he smoothed out the rhythm, and eliminated the high notes which had been mainly responsible for the wrong accents:

[1] Translation by Henry S. Drinker.

Wer nie sein Brot mit Trä - nen aß, wer nie die kum - mer-
vol - len Näch - te auf sei - nem Bet - te wei - nend saß,

etc.

Then, feeling a more dramatic interpretation to be essential, he found a curious way of expressing the greater emotional tension of the second stanza without essentially changing its strophic shape: with a sudden, very striking modulation he moved into another key, F sharp minor, gaining an extraordinary change of colour, but with the result that now, exactly transposed, the second stanza sank by another minor third to the key of E flat minor, the farthest possible distance from the original key, A minor. To proceed from here to an ending that could round off the song satisfactorily was a problem indeed! He tried to solve it by repeating the first two lines of the first stanza, thus giving himself the extra space to build, with somewhat forcible tonal moves, a final section of the song.

The result is problematic. On consideration, one would rather give preference to the first, simpler, version, in spite of its prosodic shortcomings. The second setting seems too contrived; in trying to correct one error, the composer has committed another, more serious one. He laid both of them aside. In a third version he found a glorious solution to the problem by abandoning the metrical rhythm in the second line, and giving the words free rein to follow their natural accentuation:

Wer nie sein Brot mit Trä - nen aß, wer
nie die kum - mer - vol - len Näch - te

This is not only magnificent declamation, with that unity of words and melody which characterises the true *lied*, but it also widens the somewhat narrow phrase-structure of the two previous settings, and avoids being restricted to a rigidly scanned iambic metre.

The direct consequence, however, is that the expressive phrase, just because it was so individually matched to the first two lines, became unusable later on, and thus the whole formal scheme had to be fundamentally altered. The second stanza now called for a new invention, following the word accents as closely as the first had done. The incomparably richer melodic material thereby gained now overflows the banks of the poem so that its eight lines are no longer sufficient, but must be freely repeated in order to provide the necessary substance for so much music. Thus the composer, has, in fact, returned to the unconcerned freedom with which the aria-composer formerly treated his text. At this stage of his development, paradoxically, Schubert has no hesitation in pulling a poem to pieces, dissolving the verse form into prose, as it were, in order to bring it in his own way to its fullest expressiveness. One can understand why a poet should object to such a procedure! The blatant contradiction between the composer's lack of respect for the form of the poem and his deep feeling for its content which is revealed by this method, is explained by his youth and by the total novelty of the problem. A few years later he would have done it differently; with growing experience he was to learn to preserve the form of the poem he set, and even to gain an artistic advantage from doing it full justice.

In his last setting of the Harpist's Song he used a device which had not yet occurred to him in the two previous ones: the figure of the harpist is vividly symbolised by a discreetly introduced arpeggio—his harp—which dominates the accompaniment. Such a procedure is a fairly obvious one and had been used before Schubert. What he really discovered is the structural potential of such a descriptive "tone-poetic" accompanying motif, whose formative energy can help to shape the whole song. This is true of "Gretchen am Spinnrade", where the whole composition seems to have arisen from the characteristic motif in the piano accompaniment suggesting the rotating spinning wheel, and is equally true of such powerful creations as "An Schwager Kronos" or "Gruppe aus dem Tartarus". However much the flowing melody of the voice may prevail for the listener, it is the accompaniment which, more often than the layman would suspect, lays the foundation out of which the invention grows. From a technical point of view, a Schubert *lied* is a duo for voice and instrument. Just as in an ideal performance the partner at the piano will always be both *dux* and *comes*, leader and accompanist, so in the composition itself the instrumental motif and its further development may often have been the primary idea directing the melodic line of the voice. It goes without saying that in the perfect work of art the two form an indissoluble unity.

With the subject of tone-poetic imagery an important point has been touched upon. First of all, the concept must be cleared of certain prejudices that have grown out of dubious associations. We have to understand a simple fact: musical imagery has a legitimate place in vocal music. When the words that are sung express an image, it is natural for the music to react in a descriptive way. This is why, ever since the madrigalists of the sixteenth century, poetic conceptions have influenced the formation of vocal music. Nothing could be more thoughtless than to use the term "programme music" for this, as has often been done. A "programme" only became necessary when there were attempts to apply concrete extra-musical ideas to *instrumental* music, since these can obviously never be understood without the help of explanation and commentary. But tone poetry, on the other hand, pertains to the very nature of vocal music, as it necessarily deals with extra-musical associations and the singer's words guide the listeners' imagination in the most natural manner.

In this connection an important circumstance has to be mentioned which, curiously enough, is often not fully understood. One must distinguish between an attempt to imitate an acoustic phenomenon musically, of which the most obvious and crude example is thunder in music representing a storm, and the symbolisation of an optical phenomenon by a somehow corresponding musical event, such as, for example, the depiction of the lightning preceding the thunder by a shrill, jagged figure in the high woodwinds. The aesthetically questionable nature of the whole procedure is demonstrated by the fact that, even in the most primitive and frequent manifestation of descriptive music, the representation of a thunderstorm, two different languages, sound-imitation and symbolism, are indiscriminately mixed.

Since acoustic events that are suitable for musical imitation are relatively rare, except for the ever-popular bird-songs, symbolism predominates in descriptive music. The brook in the second movement of Beethoven's Pastoral Symphony, or in Schubert's *Schöne Müllerin*, is an example of a simple musical symbol which, too, had already long been conventional: the visible movement of the waves is translated into an undulating motif; similarly the rotating motion of Gretchen's spinning wheel is symbolised by an evenly rotating passage in the piano accompaniment. We respond to such tone-poetic images because we have been unconsciously conditioned to them by experience. The galloping rider in "Erlkönig", Gretchen's spinning wheel, the rippling brook in "Wohin", the graceful curve of "The Trout" in the clear water, the stormy night in "Die junge Nonne", are tone-symbols that no listener can fail to understand. In Schubert's songs they always have a double function: they provide a vividly pictorial background, and give unity to the composition as adaptable, constructive accompanying motifs. This device replaced Zumsteeg's dubious ballad form which disintegrates into small episodes; but such an achievement demanded the unlimited melodic invention and the far-reaching harmonic horizon which Schubert brought into the song as his most personal contributions.

His struggle for mastery was long and hard. Anyone who thinks it strange that the young artist's strokes of genius should stand amidst a thicket of total or partial failures, mediocre and poor products, should try to imagine the situation of a youthful adept who has to steal every hour he devotes to his beloved art from the stultifying occupation by which he earns his living.

Sometimes one almost has the impression that he is going round in circles. Over and over again he succumbs to the temptation to do the obvious, to take the easy way out with the strophic song, or to use Zumsteeg's expedient of a pseudo-form. Thus on a single day, 19 August 1815, the eighteen-year-old wrote five songs to Goethe poems. One of them, "Heidenröslein", has become immortal. The others, "An den Mond", "Der Rattenfänger", "Der Schatzgräber", "Bundeslied", may be counted among his writing exercises. And he manages to write strophic songs whose very idea seems monstrous until we remember that the song as it came down to Schubert was a type of social entertainment, as the passage from Rousseau explains so amusingly. "Idens Schwanenlied", a poem by Kosegarten, has no less than seventeen stanzas. Even more horrifying is a setting of Körner's "Schwertlied", consisting of sixteen stanzas, each of which culminates in a thrice-repeated "Hurrah", sung by the choir, to which the composer adds in brackets: "At 'Hurrah' clanging of swords." Then again one finds rhapsodic pieces of Zumsteegian bombast, recognisable at the first glance from their inserted bits of recitativo. Yet at that time Schubert already had "Gretchen am Spinnrade" behind him! It is as if he had again lost the key which, as if by a miracle, he had once held in his hand. But then, in close succession, come three magnificent pieces: "Erlkönig", "An Schwager Kronos" and "Der Wanderer", and now the worst is over, although still not without occasional relapses. These are by no means due to any lack of critical faculties. It is in the nature of the *lied* as Schubert conceived it that it does not recognise any fixed norm. The poem makes it own demands; the problem is a new one each time, and can only be solved individually through the composer's ever-growing awareness of its implications.

What makes Schubert's monumental songs so impressive is just that for which he had striven so hard: the combination of a clearly organised, richly contrasted form and an unconstrained spontaneity of expression. I have already mentioned how decisively a descriptive motif in the accompaniment may influence the formal structure. This is totally different in kind from unsophisticated pictorial details such as occur as marginal vignettes in Haydn's "Creation"—the lion, the stag, the worm —or in Beethoven's Klärchen Song, "The drums are beating, the fifes shrilly play", from Goethe's *Egmont*. With Schubert similar things only happen in the most immature attempts of his Zumsteeg-period. Anything that one may call tone-poetic in his *lied* became part of its substance, its cell structure.

The manner in which this is achieved differs individually according to the composer's response to the poem. Gretchen's spinning wheel is the background to her song; she sings as she spins. But the motif of the rotating wheel, first appearing as the background, is transformed into a surging wave of sound when she breaks into rapturous enthusiasm—"Sein hoher Gang, sein' edle Gestalt" ("His noble air, his gallant mien")—and at the climax of her ecstasy—"Und ach, sein Kuss!" ("And ah, his kiss!")—the wheel stops, and only after a pause, haltingly, is it set in motion again. This is purest poetry, recreated in music by the composer's imagination. How immeasurably he has transcended the expressive limits of the words becomes clear when one realises how much more emotionally restrained a spoken recitation would have to be, if it were not to appear intolerably exaggerated. In poetry, whose only tool is the word, thought is in control; in music, on the other hand, feeling and emotion predominate, and this explains the enormously enlarged range of expression achieved by the conjunction of these two media.

Whereas in "Gretchen" a lyrical mood prevails, expressed in a flowing vocal line, "Erlkönig" is driven by a dramatic impulse which nowhere permits the repetition of a word or a line, yet always leaves enough space to evoke a vivid picture of what the poet's concise words leave to the imagination. Beginning and end are narrative, everything in between is in the form of a dialogue, and this is so gripping in its characterisation, so penetrating in its tonal gesture, as to give the characters an uncanny reality. Here for the first time Schubert has discovered a vocal style that combines the declamatory energy of recitativo with the form-giving symmetry of the arioso. Here, too, the accompaniment asserts its dominant position. The stormy triplet motif of the ritornello, which remains a unifying element throughout, symbolises rider, night and wind. It gallops through the whole ballad until, close to the final catastrophe, it suddenly comes to a halt. The reduction of the texture to a terse recitativo phrase, dryly stating the fact—"In seinen Armen das Kind war tot" ("In his arms the child was dead")—is unparalleled in its dramatic impact. The singer who tries to heighten the effect by pathos or sentiment has failed to understand the idea. Here again we are confronted with the phenomenon of an emotional intensification arising from the combination of words and music, such as Schubert achieved time and again in a unique way. It is as though the poet's thought and feeling, absorbed by the composer's responsive imagination, had been reborn into a new, immeasurably richer existence.

"An Schwager Kronos" is a magnificent allegory, an extraordinary transformation of an abstract idea into a visual panorama. The image of Kronos, the God of Time, as a postillion hurriedly driving us through life in his bumpy coach, is Goethe's most outstanding vision of this kind. It is perhaps the only mythologically inspired poem which is purely pictorial, without any overt moral or aesthetic leanings, without any philosophical or didactic digression. It was this freshness of perception, wedded to depth of thought, which delighted the musician. And what he made of it is so great that it almost defies a perfect rendering.

The rhapsodic poem with its constantly changing metre—the young Goethe actually wrote it down while travelling in a mail-coach—stimulates the emergence of an equally rhapsodic vocal style. Here again the form is energetically welded together by a brilliantly vital and adaptable accompanying motif, a staccato figure which, pushed by hard, accentuated leading-notes, presses intrepidly upwards regardless of all obstacles:

> Frisch, holpert es gleich,
> Über Stock und Steine den Trott
> Rasch ins Leben hinein!

> (On then, though the carriage jolts,
> Trot over sticks and stones
> Quickly out into life!)

Thus, driving impetuously onwards, it climbs uphill in chromatically rising modulations. But then we arrive at the summit:

> Weit, hoch, herrlich der Blick
> Rings ins Leben hinein,
> Vom Gebirg zum Gebirg
> Schwebet der ewige Geist,
> Ewigen Lebens ahndevoll.

> (Far, high, glorious the view
> Around into life,
> From mountain to mountain
> Hovers the eternal spirit,
> Sensing eternal life.)

There is nothing like it in the whole of music. We breathe mountain air, see before us the view from a high ridge. And here the music also finds the necessary breathing space for lyrical expansion, the only one in this song, for an inexpressibly tender idyll, caught, as it were, in a snapshot:

> Seitwärts des Überdachs Schatten
> Zieht dich an
> Und ein Frischung verheissender Blick
> Auf der Schwelle des Mädchens da.
> Labe dich!—Mir auch, Mädchen,
> Diesen schäumenden Trank,
> Diesen frischen Gesundheitsblick!

> (Sideways the shadow of shelter
> Draws you on,
> And the eyes of the girl
> At the doorway promise refreshment.
> Be comforted!—For me too, girl,
> This foaming drink,
> This fresh gaze of health!)

Then, however, the traveller goes quickly down on the other side, descending inexorably to the abyss:

> Sieh, die Sonne sinkt!

> (Look, the sun is sinking!)

Without sorrow or regret, with the same magnificent clarity of view that has guided him through life, he sees the end before him:

> Töne, Schwager, ins Horn,
> Rassle den schallenden Trab,
> Dass der Orkus vernehme: wir kommen,
> Dass gleich an der Türe
> Der Wirt uns freundlich empfange.

(Coachman, sound your horn,
Let the resounding trot rattle,
So that the underworld sees we are coming,
So that right at the doors
The landlord, friendly, receive us.)[1]

The postillion sounds his horn; we have arrived at the goal to which every human life leads.

One must not compare such greatness of conception with a third-rate poem such as "Der Wanderer" by Georg Philipp Schmidt von Lübeck, which owes its survival solely to Schubert's music. He has sometimes been accused of a lack of literary taste. Unjustly so. He understood the quality of a poem better than any of his critics. He did not miss a single poet of importance available to him, from Klopstock and Ossian to the first, newly published poems by Heine, which happened to come into his hands. But his demand for poetry was insatiable, and when he did not find a Goethe poem which suited his mood—he set seventy-two of them—he had to content himself with authors such as Rellstab, Kosegarten, Jacobi, Schubart, Rochlitz, or his friend Mayrhofer, who, by the way, was no mean poet. Schubert set forty-eight of his poems.

Here a question arises which has frequently been the subject of arguments and has caused misunderstandings and misjudgments. In a song which is a masterpiece, must the poem be equal in stature to the music? If one puts the question in this form, the answer is bound to be negative: one glance at the works, say, of Schubert or Brahms will suffice to demonstrate this. Both have created magnificent songs with poems which even the most benevolent judge could not call anything but second-rate. However, this by no means clarifies the problem. One comes nearer to it by examining an assertion that has actually been made, namely that a competent composer should be able to set even a menu to music. No doubt he could do this; the only question is what such a composition would be like. The artist is master of his craft but he cannot command his imagination, which only becomes really creative when it is appropriately stimulated. Though there are undoubtedly inferior poems which have become immortal songs, no such

[1] Translation by David McDuff.

song has ever been created without the composer's having drawn a genuine inspiration from the poetic subject. A thought, a feeling, a single word can set the mysterious mechanism in motion from which an invention is born, and Schubert's unsurpassably rich source of inspiration was always ready to flow.

Alongside this direct emotional reaction, however, there is another, conscious one. The composer who is a genuine lyricist and to whose spiritual world poetry belongs, will easily be upset by a clumsy line, a commonplace rhyme, or a wrong image; and such disillusionment may hinder or impair the spontaneous action of his imagination, whereas true poetry, appealing to the musician's sensibility, becomes a mighty stimulus to his inspiration and engenders his richest inventions. This is the reason why a vocal composer's greatest achievements are so frequently based on poetical works of congenial greatness. This is undoubtedly the case with Schubert, and in this respect his relationship to Goethe is unequivocal. In a similar way Hugo Wolf attained the summit of his achievement with his Goethe and Mörike settings.

Quite apart from such considerations, an aesthetic problem must not be judged in isolation. A song does not stand in a vacuum; it addresses itself to a singer and a listener. If the latter has a feeling for genuine artistic perfection—and in pondering over such a question one is justified in considering only the most highly qualified performer and listener, as well as an ideal clarity of enunciation—a master's setting of a supremely great poem will be an unsurpassable experience.

Schubert has proved that he was capable of such discrimination. But, like every true lyricist, he was very dependent not only on his literary taste but on his mood and his expressive urge, both of which will have varied at different times and were decisive as to whether a poem could seize him and make him productive at any given moment. "Der Wanderer" went to his heart. How deeply the poem moved him is reflected in the inspiration he drew from it. This song was not only a favourite with his friends, right from the beginning, but it became the source of one of his greatest piano works. The song also deserves attention for its rare and curious formal design. Since the poetic image changes from one couplet to the next, the composer felt that a continuous pattern running right through the accompaniment would be out of place. He moves from episode to episode, with changes of key, time and speed, and this results in no less than five differently-organised lyrical inventions of which only one eventually reappears as a recapitulation. The only perceptible formative principle in this continuous change of aspect is a heightening of expressiveness up to a climax and a descent to the recapitulation of the melodic episode mentioned above. Is this a last offshoot of the discarded Zumsteegian form? If so, it has outgrown it immeasurably. Whatever comes so directly from Schubert's heart and soul is irresistible; and in such a case his natural instinct for form always arrives at a convincing construction.

With such an impetuous creative drive, it is difficult to believe that he had any systematic method. It seems, though, that productivity is always governed by certain regulating forces, of which the artist himself may not necessarily be aware. One such organising principle is the urge to fill the given space in every direction. There is no type of poem on which Schubert did not try his hand, no verse form which he did not learn to master in his own way. In this respect one of his most amazing achievements is his setting of Pyrker's poem "Das Heimweh", one of his most monumental *lied*-creations. Here he even succeeded in breaking the hexameter, the stiffest, musically most unmanageable of all metrical patterns, into a spontaneous, easy flow of melody. And when he had become conscious of his mastery, attained in years of indefatigable effort, he turned to another intractable problem, large-scale instrumental composition, with which he had hitherto only toyed. This does not mean that he at any time neglected the song. It remained omnipresent, interspersed everywhere among the great instrumental works of his later years. During the last ten years of his life he hardly wrote a single song that does not bear his personal stamp. There may have been practical reasons for the fact that during this period when the harvest of his works was so overwhelmingly rich, the grandiose *lied*-creations like "Ganymed", "Prometheus", "Grenzen der Menschheit", "Der Zürnenden Diana", "Heimweh", "Die Allmacht", take second place beside the more intimate, lyrical type of song; it was easier to find a publisher for smaller, less demanding pieces, and Schubert was desperately dependent upon publication.

It has already been pointed out that at Schubert's time a public performance of songs was a rare and rather exceptional event. Since then, of course, this most intimate type of music has long taken its place on the concert platform alongside all the other forms of chamber and domestic music. This was an inevitable development whose sociological background does not need to be discussed here. But the essential feature of the *lied* is explained by its original intimate form: its simple, unobtrusive character, not designed for effect. A talented singer like Michael Vogl soon found out that with a Schubert song, too, he could impress an audience.

This effect, however, is due to expressive execution, not to vocal virtuosity. The majority of Schubert's songs demand a minimum of vocal display. They were written for the singing and playing amateurs of which there were so many among the educated middle class in Vienna, for those circles to which the Schubertians belonged. One sang them for oneself or possibly at a social gathering. The difference between this way of singing and the expansive vocal style of opera is obvious, and not only in comparison with the Italian, the Rossinian brilliance, but also with the far less virtuosic demands of Weber's operatic roles. There are a great many Schubert songs—among them such well-known ones as "Frühlingsglaube", "Nähe des Geliebten", "Heidenröslein", "Das Wandern", "Danksagung an den Bach", "Tränenregen", "Die liebe Farbe", "Trockne Blumen", "Ave Maria", "Sei mir gegrüsst"—in which the range of the vocal part does not exceed a ninth. It may seem curious that in the majority of cases it is actually the ninth, not the octave. This, however, is due to organic conditions of a natural melodic structure. Mediaeval theorists already knew of the *subsemitonium*, the leading note below the tonic, as an important step for the shaping of a cadence, which in the higher register is matched, as in a mirror, by the upper second. The octave or the ninth are the usual compass of folksong, and it is fully in keeping with this that a popular figure such as Mozart's Papageno hardly oversteps this limit in his songs, one of which was quoted above. It may have contributed to the early success of Schubert's melodies that they show a certain affinity with folksong in this respect, and that they do not exceed the limits of a modestly trained voice. That they demand of the singer special qualities of the highest order, quite apart from an understanding of their emotional depth, is, of course, a different matter altogether. Of this Schubert himself was hardly aware. An essentially new art required a new kind of presentation which could only be evolved in practice, and this applies most particularly to the songs of his late period, which are so totally concentrated on expression.

The main types of form to be found there are either basically strophic with certain variations in detail where necessary, or an alternation of strophe and antistrophe, a different, contrasting episode, such as is found in an instrumental rondo, or a combination of both. Schubert had developed his feeling for the expressive shade of every word to a still higher degree than in his earlier period, even drawing an unexpected advantage from the occasional necessity of changing a melodic detail in accordance with the poetic meaning. Similar things occur when Mozart, in a transposed recapitulation, arrives at the limit of an instrument's compass, and, being compelled to change a melodic phrase, enriches it in the subtlest manner. With Schubert such moments always have an immediate impact, because they are connected with a significantly articulated word, and because it is precisely by the deviation from the shape of the melody as we have heard it before that such an expressive moment becomes still more impressive. Sometimes it is an obvious symbol which causes an alteration, as in Rochlitz's poem "Alinde", where in the third stanza the composer feels obliged to replace a descending phrase by an ascending one:

(a) "The sun sinks into the deep blue sea."
(b) "The brilliant stars are rising high."

Such little touches show the conscious care with which the songwriter, a real miniaturist, deals with every detail. In "Gute Nacht", the introduction of *Winterreise*, the alterations of an otherwise strophically treated melody are all connected with subtleties of expression. The cunning with which the composer has solved a prosodic problem in this song deserves special attention. In the first stanza, and again in the last, the stressed opening syllable conflicts with the iambic metre ∪‿, which demands a weak upbeat. Translators have rightly smoothed out such awkward problems for the singer. The situation in the German original will be understood from the following, admittedly clumsy, translation:

> ∪ –∪ – ∪ –∪ –
> Lonely as was my entry here,
> ∪ –∪ – ∪ –
> lonely again I go.

The composer resolves this conflict by putting the first upbeat on a higher note, thus neutralising the inappropriate regular accentuation of the bar. Thus at every recapitulation of the melodic phrase a discreet emphasis can be obtained, according to whether the word accent is with or against the scansion, by utilising the advantage of either the higher note or the strong beat:

With this expedient all prosodic problems were solved, and a strophic setting of the whole poem would have been feasible. That the composer did not carry it through is proof of the poetic sensibility with which he had learnt to approach such a task. For the second stanza he used a strophic repetition. But in the third he made a number of changes, as he felt that the quietly flowing melody was no longer suited to the more intense expression of the words. And in the fourth and last stanza the lonely, melancholy sceptic has overwhelmingly warm and expressive moments. The structure of the stanza is unaffected, but it has moved to the major key, and with some slight variations of detail the melody has gained an indescribable tenderness of feeling:

Will dich im Traum nicht stö - ren, wär schad' um dei - ne___ Ruh,

When, towards the end, with a repeat of the last line, "An dich hab ich gedacht" ("On you my thoughts did rest")—the only extension of the stanza beyond its original shape—the music relapses into the minor key, with the hopeless depressiveness of the beginning, depths of the soul are revealed that raise a small song to the region of sublimity. And this introduction to the song cycle is matched by its end, the most poignant expression of a destroyed soul that there has ever been. Never has human ruin been represented more hauntingly than it is here, negatively, by what is *not* said. Once again the singer must be warned against any over-emphasis; only the utmost simplicity of expression can succeed in making such agony an artistic experience. Nothing is more admirable than Schubert's artistic instinct, his tact in avoiding any emotional overstatement. His means of communication is melody, and this does not permit exaggeration or distortion.

It may be mentioned that the major and minor keys as symbols of the light and dark sides of our emotional spectrum, a result of modern dual tonality, are as deeply rooted in romantic music as they were previously in classical and pre-classical style. We must assume that this principle rests on a universal emotional response. Exceptions prove the rule: the funeral march in C major in Handel's *Saul* is considered a curiosity. From the polar opposition of major and minor Schubert developed one of the most specific features of his harmonic idiom, not only as a natural means of expression in the juxtaposition of the two modes, but by discovering, beyond this, wide extensions of the tonal range (of which more will be said later). In song, where the emotional situation is expressed in words, simple characterisation by the mode can be found everywhere. A particularly striking case of its humorous use is the song "Lachen und Weinen" ("Laughing and Crying"), because the relationship between these and major and minor is so obvious. In "Gute Nacht", the opening of *Winterreise*, Schubert uses this commonplace device in a far subtler way. The personal grief of the lonely, melancholy sufferer is brought into contact with the tender warmth of genuine love, and the icy armour of the minor key melts away at its touch.

Here we have arrived at a decisive point which applies to both song cycles, *Die schöne Müllerin* and *Winterreise*. Written in 1823 and 1827 respectively, they represent the song-writer at the summit of his powers. It has often been stated that they are still greater in their entirety than in their component parts, and, though this is intended as praise, it contains an intimation that, if we judge these songs critically, we will not be able to rank some of them, taken individually, with the greatest of Schubert's achievements, with works such as "Sei mir gegrüsst", "Du bist die Ruh", "Ständchen", the two "Suleika" songs, "Geheimes", "Der Doppelgänger", "Am Meer", not to mention the great Goethe settings discussed earlier. But the assertion is correct. One has to view the two cycles as a whole in order fully to appreciate the individual style which so naturally unifies each cycle, their splendid arrangement and their irresistible emotional appeal. *Die schöne Müllerin* is an amiable, easy-going idyll until after the middle, when suddenly—"Der Jäger" and "Eifersucht und Stolz" are hardly sufficient for such a transition—it turns into tragedy. And in *Winterreise*, which dispenses with any action and confines itself to lyrical contemplation, the self-tormenting obsession of the hero is a perpetual state of mind, and all contrast is restricted to changes in the external surroundings.

Wilhelm Müller, the poet of the two cycles—he died almost as young as Schubert, who made him immortal—was a respected poet, and his writing has the virtues of fluent diction and smooth form. What he lacks is depth of thought and expression, and his lachrymose sentimentality is a fashionable stylistic feature which has made so many literary products of German romanticism difficult to swallow. Schubert, his brother Ferdinand, and their circle of friends were by no means free from this type of sentimentality, and in their correspondence tears are a frequent event. If one glances over the poems of *Die schöne Müllerin*, they have little appeal, and this holds true not only of "Tränenregen" ("Floods of Tears"), as one of them is actually called.

To see beyond the threadbare texture of these lyrics, the banality of a story which one would call pitiful rather than tragic, one must look with the eyes of Schubert, whom the fate of the young miller moved so deeply. This miller is a silly youth. One feels sorry for him, and impatient with his defencelessness, and that is all. And the hero of *Winterreise* has not even the appeal of simplicity which makes the young miller worthy of sympathy. The winter traveller's *Weltschmerz* is not without an element of pose; it is a kind of conceited pride, the melancholy of an intellectual who knows what is expected of a young romantic.

What glory Schubert has conjured into these poems! *He* is the poet who, with feelings of unfathomable depth, has turned the pretence of second-hand poetry into burning reality. Through him the insipid young miller has become a live human being who suffers unspeakable grief.

All the same, Schubert did not entirely escape the homespun simplicity contained in the verses of *Die schöne Müllerin*. However poetic "Wohin" may be, however irresistible the enthusiasm of "Ungeduld", the jubilation of "Mein!", Schubert at his greatest only reveals himself at the approach of the tragic climax. With "Die liebe Farbe" ("The Favourite Colour"— the title is meant ironically) we have entered a new world. This is Schubert with his unique capacity to feel the agony of an afflicted soul. "Mein Schatz hat's Grün so gern" ("My Love's so fond of green"): green is the colour of his rival, the huntsman, the colour that means death to him; green is his obsession, symbolised by a single note, F sharp, which pulsates incessantly throughout the piece, quietly and insidiously. Like most of these songs—in this the composer accepted the stylised folksong character of the poems—this one too is strophic, a simple sixteen-bar melody, with an introductory ritornello which already sounds that ominous F sharp. No other strophic song has such expressive power, effected by repetition, usually the constitutional weakness of strophic form. Both halves of the symmetrically-constructed melody of the two eight-bar phrases form their cadence in the same peculiar manner, with the major third, D sharp, in the accompaniment, sinking in the following bar to D natural, the minor third—a moment of heart-rending tragedy:

D

Elsewhere Schubert would achieve his most expressive effects by melodic variation; here he does it through insistent repetition. Twice in each stanza, six times in all, the terrible moment arrives; one awaits it anxiously, and every time it pierces the heart. Nowhere in the whole of music has an obsessive thought, with all its inexorable cruelty, been portrayed like this. One feels that this man is doomed. From then onwards the gulf between the insipidity of the poems and the depth of feeling of the music becomes wider and wider. We have to cling to the latter. When at the end the brook sings a lullaby for the unfortunate youth who has found his rest, one recognises once again that there is no sorrow which Schubert could not dissolve into melody, and no triviality which could not be transformed into the purest work of art when his music streams over it.

The case of *Winterreise* is even more involved. There are many who shy away from it. When I was younger I did not understand the reason. Today I know better: a full identification with the mental state reflected in this unique work is an emotional experience against which a healthy instinct rebels. "Dass mir vor meiner Jugend graut" ("I have a horror of my youth") . . . "Wie weit noch bis zum Grabe" ("How far still to my grave?") . . . "Jeder Strom wird's Meer gewinnen, jedes Leiden auch sein Grab" ("Every stream must reach the ocean, every sorrow finds its tomb"). . . . This is an abysmal weariness of life which almost evokes a sense of embarrassment. Here and there the poet's words unmistakably suggest an undertone of tragic irony. What the music portrays is naked despair. To surrender to such feelings as an addict indulges in his narcotic is a temptation for the lyricist who, when stirred to the depth of his soul, is capable of conjuring up a world of beauty from his emotion. Here Schubert's art of melodic invention has brought forth its choicest, rarest, most magnificent blossoms. How wisely the few less darkly toned episodes, such as "Der Lindenbaum", "Frühlingstraum", "Die Post", are distributed! How moving are these very moments when the melancholic's will to live still finds the illusion of consolation! And how inimitable is the art of the tone-poet, to whom the poet's imagery—"Gefrorne Tränen" ("Frozen tears"), "Es bellen die Hunde" ("The dogs are barking"), "Die Wetterfahne" ("The weather vane")—has suggested plastic musical symbols, growing into fascinating inventions!

The choice of a subject with such obvious dangers indicates the irresistible attraction which desperate moods of this kind held for Schubert at this period. His friends have told us of the deep depression into which he fell while working at *Winterreise*. Most probably this was a confusion of cause and effect. But who knows the enigma of the soul, the enigma of the will to live and its disintegration? *Winterreise* may have drawn Schubert even more unresistingly to the abyss to which he was so near. On his death-bed he read the proofs of these songs. This was his last work, the object of his last thoughts.

The crisis of subjectivity on which romanticism was in the end to founder can already be discerned here in its beginnings: the conflict between unrestrained abandonment to one's feelings and instinctive resistance to such abandonment. One is reminded of *Tristan*, an opposite pole in the development of romanticism. In this work Wagner, as a dramatist, succeeded in objectifying his own inner crisis, and thus in liberating himself from it. He was more robust, and could overcome the crisis, emerging from it safe and sound. The lyricist was destroyed by it.

Undoubtedly there is also an aesthetic problem involved to which an answer has to be found. Every work of art contains its own implicit ideal of realisation, suggested by its character. The lyrical episodes of *Die schöne Müllerin* tell a coherent story; they form a sequence of happenings which, like a drama, lead, according to the classical definition, through the tragic experience to *katharsis*, the purifying of the soul through fear and pity. And this, too, like any drama, is directed towards a community that participates in the event with sorrow and sympathy. But *Winterreise* is a lonely, personal utterance, an extended monologue that would naturally eschew any witness. To a sensitive listener a public exhibition of such personal feelings appears almost like a profanation. Strictly speaking, this work, with all it implies, will only be experienced in its fullest sense by someone who sings and plays it for himself in lonely seclusion, or who can gain the illusion of such a perfect identification with it through an ideal rendering. He who is able to experience it with all his soul will be close to tears, and if he cannot suppress them he will find himself in good company.

5

THE GREAT INSTRUMENTAL WORKS

WHAT HAS BEEN said so far should suffice to refute the assumption, so firmly rooted in the *Schwammerl*-legend, that Schubert was an inspired somnambulist with no intellectual capacity or critical consciousness. Such a view cannot be reconciled with the profundity which one encounters everywhere in Schubert's major works. Yet it is undeniable that with him the spontaneous inventive impulse was always the initial act, and its critical control only secondary.

This is, of course, true in principle of any genuine artistic achievement, however much it may vary in degree. With Beethoven and Brahms the creative invention is immediately combined with a critical awareness of its quality and fertility. With Schubert, this act of control seems to follow at some distance, and he does not always appear to be inclined to draw the necessary conclusions from it. This can be attributed not only to his youth but also to his mode of working, which has already been mentioned. Under the pressure of irksome obligations he adopted the habit of hastily putting down on paper what would otherwise have been in danger of being submerged by humdrum duties, and thus evaporating. This was how he worked right to the end of his life.

His development as an instrumental composer follows his ascent to mastery as a song-writer at a considerable distance, but under essentially similar conditions. Here, too, before the artist finally finds his own way, there are early masterpieces and numerous relapses into questionable and obstinately persistent patterns which he had seemed already to have overcome. The two developments overlap: the first mature instrumental works coincide with the peak achievements of the *lied*-composer, and it is not until his mid-twenties that Schubert has fully outgrown his instrumental apprenticeship.

It is clear that his total absorption in the problems of song-writing, and the specific approach to form which stemmed from this, had a decisive influence on his whole mode of inven-

tion. No doubt we may link with his self-taught development
the fact that he tackled each kind of composition with the same
unprejudiced approach that had been so successful with the
lied: diligent practical work. This does not imply that he did
not learn from the work of his predecessors. But their influence
was more or less limited to externals. The principle of symphonic form which he took from the classics hardly meant
more to him than a well-tried constructional method, from
which he could see no cogent reason to depart, and which
offered a rich supply of models that were worth following. The
example of Beethoven, whose greatness fascinated him more
and more compellingly as he grew in maturity, could in some
respects show him the way. But what stood between them was
not only a fundamental incompatibility of character, but an
age-difference of twenty-seven years which, under the peculiar
conditions of the period, involved a step over the threshold of a
new age. Beethoven, the form-conscious classicist, was opposed
by a new, transformed world: that process of fermentation
called romanticism had begun. The difference in age between
Haydn and Mozart was almost as great, but in no way did it
have a comparable effect.

To classicism belongs a firm control of the expressive component by the form-conscious mind. Schubert's generation was
the first to abandon such discipline. But it is an unproven
assertion that romantic expressiveness and a disciplined sense of
form need be mutually exclusive. Music without form is unthinkable. Genuine romantics such as Mendelssohn, Schumann,
or Chopin were extremely form-conscious, not to mention
Brahms, who combined the expressive urge of a romantic with
an unsurpassable sense of classical form. In the other camp, it
is true, stand the rebels against form, such as Berlioz or Liszt;
their works, however, sufficiently demonstrate the aesthetic
problems inherent in this attitude. The crux of the matter is
that romantic exuberance is liable to brim over the vessel of
form and that an ideal balance between the two components
is therefore difficult to find. In this respect all the great masters
had to find their own salvation. With Chopin the result was
the miniature, whose ultimate conclusion can be admired in
his preludes, which he shaped with such an exquisite sense of
form. With Schubert the opposite happened. In his hands the

slender classical form had to endure considerable expansion in order to provide the necessary space for an emotional extravagance for which it had not been created. His expressive urge finds its outlet in lingering on a beautiful moment, enhancing it by repetition, returning to it again and again.

What arises from this is a certain indifference towards basic principles of concise shaping, an indifference manifesting itself not in formlessness but, quite the reverse, in formalism. In a construction which is determined by episodes of intense expression, these being the most essential content of the composition, form is in danger of becoming merely a practical device instead of an architectural design. To put it differently: the romantic makes use of the well-tried solidity of a certain groundplan without concerning himself with the deeper architectural idea inherent in it. Schubert's form is often schematic, more a product of acquired habit than of deep organic motivation; this cannot be doubted, and there is no point in denying it. He adopted classical form because he could not envisage any other structural principle. But its dynamic demand for vigorous thematic confrontation is incompatible with the lyricist's tendency to linger on a beautiful moment; he relaxes this dynamic tension by turning it into something static. Vocally-conceived, almost song-like main subjects, episodic developments, and practically unchanged recapitulations are characteristics of Schubert's form. But what his works lose in dynamic tension they make up for in lyrical expansiveness and an abundant wealth of richly chiselled detail. Whoever sees the loss without noticing the gain may be inclined to underrate Schubert, although this could hardly happen without total insensitivity to his most magnificent and most personal contribution, and a lack of feeling for a grandeur and originality of conception that will bear comparison with any of the greatest.

When a young artist has, at an early stage, acquired a facility of invention and shaping, his foremost aim is to develop a personal style. This holds true of young Schubert, as of any beginner. With his usual haste in writing, uninhibited by reflection, in his early compositions he did not often succeed in allowing a large-scale work of several movements the necessary time to mature in all its parts without some lapse or inadequacy. Much of what he wrote during his adolescence is undistinguished, and there are remarkably many unfinished works—a peculiar, ominous phenomenon which will be thoroughly discussed later. Of ten piano sonatas begun between his eighteenth and twentieth birthdays only three were finished; the others remained fragments. Everywhere striking, original inventions can be found alongside conventional ones, not only when one compares different compositions but even different movements of the same work. This is just as applicable to the symphonies of these transitional years, his Fourth, Fifth, and Sixth, as to his numerous early string quartets. Schubert was no infant prodigy. But the same could be said of Beethoven, who wrote his first fully mature music at the age of twenty-three: the three glorious piano trios which he published as his Opus 1, thereby proudly disowning all he had written before and relegating it unequivocally to the junk-room. Schubert would not have been any more lenient with *his* numerous juvenilia, not published till long after his death, than his great predecessor. Six immature symphonies are heavy ballast for one who had so short a time to live. They contain a profusion of graceful and lovable detail, which is sufficient to justify the occasional performance; but the distance between these early instrumental adventures and the great works that were to follow some years later is as great as that between the "exercises of the pen" and the masterpieces of the *lied* which they preceded. One also has to consider that the effort of rounding off a voluminous instrumental composition required many times the concentration and critical self-control demanded by a song.

But the genuine Schubert is to be found everywhere. In the minuet of the second of the above mentioned piano sonatas written by the eighteen-year-old Schubert, the one in E major, there is a trio whose basic idea he was able to re-use nine years later in a consummate masterpiece, his Sonata in D major, Op. 53. But he gave up this early work after three movements, without writing a finale, probably because he had become aware of shortcomings. The first movement starts with practically nothing—a mere flourish, an ascending arpeggio. Beethoven would not have written down anything as meaningless, even in a first sketch. Behind such unconcern, of which Schubert was not altogether free even at the time of his maturity, lies an unlimited confidence in the resourcefulness of his imagination; he knows it will never let him down when it comes to the crucial moment of continuing and expanding his invention. With Haydn or Beethoven, for whom every note of a main subject is of organic importance, the opening of a movement is always decisive for all that is to follow. It may occasionally be different with Mozart who, like Schubert, never seems to doubt that something strong and meaningful will be sure to come along, however non-committal the beginning may have been. What may also be involved here is the difference between the symphonic and the dramatic composer, the latter occasionally confining himself to a mere gesture. The first movement of the Jupiter Symphony is a marvel of perfection. Yet it begins with no more than a conventional formula:

Mozart succeeds in enlivening the formula when it first returns by confronting it with a counter-subject, and only now does it become symphonically strong and productive:

Such a procedure is alien to Schubert's style, and here we come up against something vitally important: Schubert does not think in a contrapuntal way. His craftsmanship, his art of part-writing, is beyond reproach, and the colourfulness of his harmony is without equal. But as far as polyphony is concerned, it is at the periphery of his style, not an essential structural component but an enrichment of the sound by additional melodic parts. His form is hardly ever determined by the vitality of a dynamic contrapuntal motif. In his songs the lay-out of voice and accompaniment is certainly not altogether homophonic: the piano may reply to a vocal phrase with a counter-motif, an imitation, or an answering remark. But only in a limited sense can this be called polyphonic, and one could say much the same of his piano writing, or his string-quartet and orchestral style, which can display magnificent sound, yet still be far distant from the sinuous tautness of a Beethoven instrumental texture. Beethoven's ideal is a Michelangelesque muscularity, Schubert's a cushion of soft, luxuriant sound. One glance at a second violin or viola part in any of their scores will confirm this assertion.

One remembers that a few weeks before his death Schubert made up his mind to take lessons in counterpoint from the Viennese Court Organist Simon Sechter. This fact has been glossed over by biographers with condescending superiority. What could a Schubert have learnt from a Sechter? Obviously nothing, if one puts the question in this way. But if Sechter could have succeeded in stimulating Schubert to come to grips with a discipline which he had hardly touched in his formative years, contrapuntal thinking and the unlimited possibilities of polyphony, it is quite conceivable that his imagination would have responded to such a stimulus with hitherto unrealised creative potentialities. The speculation as such seems idle; but it is significant that at this time, at the peak of his creative life, Schubert felt a desire to widen his horizon in this direction. Considering this, it is not blasphemy to discuss certain limi-tations in his technical range whose problematic nature is evident, if only because they have so often led to the underrating of his achievement.

Obviously one must not expect of him something alien to his nature, and must understand that it is perhaps precisely the focusing of his imagination on basically homophonic pat-terns of invention that gave rise to the unprecedented richness of his melodic and harmonic idiom, and the beauty of sound inherent in it. One cannot imagine what would have happened if an artist with such superabundant gifts, at the summit of his powers, had turned towards remote, hitherto unexplored regions. In this connection one may think of Mozart, with whom the first acquaintance with Bach's "Forty-Eight" at a decisive stage of his development brought about a fundamental reorientation of his polyphonic thinking, with profound and far-reaching effects on the work of the last eight years of his life. Just as the transparent, spiritualised counterpoint of his late symphonies, string quintets and piano concertos, *The Magic Flute* and the *Requiem* is different from Bach's, a new Schubertian polyphonic style would presumably have differed from that of his predecessors. But that so rich a style as Schubert's could have yielded the most unexpected, most miraculous fruits by the addition of such a fundamental new component seems beyond doubt.

It lies in the very nature of the problem that a sudden break-through, such as he had achieved some years before in the *lied*, with "Gretchen am Spinnrade", was impossible in the realm of instrumental music. A sonata, a symphony or a string quartet pose different problems, not merely in respect of the writing technique; the types of form contained in such a work of several movements impose their own, totally different conditions of construction. For the song-writer, the melodist, an andante or a minuet was a sufficiently familiar proposition to be mastered by him in his own manner. But the truly symphonic types of form—an opening allegro, a finale— were far more difficult to tackle. Schubert, at twenty, was so mature an artist that simple copying of style no longer came into question for him. He had to adapt the form to his own, already very personal, mode of invention and expression, and this was a different, and vastly more difficult task.

Here, too, mature and less mature products overlap. The last two of his early symphonies, his Fifth and Sixth, which in many respects still betray their youthful immaturity, stand side by side, in the same year, with the first three of his piano sonatas (published after his death as Op. 122, 147, and 164) which can be called mature, however much Schubert surpassed them a few years later. Here it must be interpolated that the opus numbers of his works are chronologically even less reliable than Beethoven's. With both composers, the opus number was added when a work was published, and this depended on practical circumstances. The last work Schubert himself gave to a publisher was his Piano Trio in E flat, Op. 100. The piano sonatas in A minor, Op. 42, and in D major, Op. 53, were written seven years later than the three mentioned above.[1] Schubert had them published because they were the best he had to offer at that time. He never lacked critical judgment with regard to his music.

In his attitude to form there are features of youthful unconcern which he shares with the young Mozart: having succeeded in writing a well-invented expositon, he may easily be satisfied with a rudimentary development and a practically unchanged, mechanically reproduced recapitulation. Mozart soon overcame this. Schubert took a considerable time to find his own solutions to such problems of form, which will have to be discussed in detail later. As to the recapitulation, the transformed, partly transposed restatement of the exposition, one often has the impression that when this point is reached Schubert's interest in the composition is flagging and he is simply trying to conclude it in the easiest way. He copies the exposition with as few changes as possible, and is also quite happy to leave it without a coda, a fuller, more circumstantial preparation for the conclusion. This is a definite weakness in formal design, since in a weighty, large-scale composition the conclusion is hardly convincing if one has already met with it before in exactly the same manner. In this respect the young Schubert reverted to a procedure which, though adequate for a slender, sonatina-like composition, would no longer do for the large type of form inaugurated by Beethoven. And at this transitional stage in his development Schubert likes to employ a rather questionable device, all the more questionable because it reduces more than a third of the composition to a faithful transposition. As the second subject and the conclusion of the exposition are in the dominant key, Schubert's device is to follow a short development with the recapitulation starting on the subdominant, with the result that a transposed but otherwise completely identical repetition of the exposition will lead without further trouble to the desired goal of ending in the tonic. He used this trick not only in the first movements of his Fifth Symphony and his Piano Sonata in B major, but even two years later, in his first great chamber music master-

[1] As long as the chronological numbers of O. E. Deutsch's Thematic Catalogue of Schubert's Works are not yet to be found in most editions, the original opus numbers offer the only convenient means of identification.

piece, the "Trout" Quintet. And in each of these cases he saved himself the trouble of writing a coda. It is by no means only the expert, form-conscious listener with a good memory who will notice this as a deficiency: in a movement in sonata form the end of the exposition is no more than an intermediate halt, a kind of semicolon; it therefore cannot take an emphatic final build-up, and its mere restatement at the end is not convincing. Therefore one always feels that there is something unsatisfactory when a large, richly developed movement concludes with no more than a transposition of this intermediate cadence, and this should be noticeable to any discriminating listener in the outer movements of the "Trout" Quintet. In the last movement Schubert achieved the *non plus ultra* of comfortable unconcern; here the exposition is immediately followed by an exactly transposed recapitulation. If the exposition is duly repeated as indicated by the composer, one will hear exactly the same thing three times in succession. The problems of formal layout could not be approached with a more casual innocence.

Anyone who is inclined to censure should take a mitigating circumstance into account: this is music that one would not wish to do without for anything in the world, music whose magic, sweeping aside any reservations as to form, makes every objection irrelevant. The same applies to another favourite of the Schubert enthusiast, which has already been mentioned: the overture to *Rosamunde*. In form it faithfully follows the Rossinian type of overture: a rich introduction, and then an exposition and a partly transposed recapitulation with, instead of a development, no more than a few bars of transition between them. It should be remembered that this formal design probably appeared for the first time in Mozart's overture to *Figaro*, and can thus claim an august lineage. And even the trick of starting a recapitulation on the subdominant in order to arrive at an exactly transposed restatement was actually invented by Mozart, who used it in his small Piano Sonata in C major, K. 545.

The questionable features of Schubert's form can be traced back to one main cause: the overriding, almost exclusive importance of the melodic substance in his creative process. No doubt he would have arrived at a more comprehensive grasp of architectural principles had he been granted a longer life, and more opportunities—this is an important point— to be objectively confronted with his music in public perform- ance. Schubert rarely had such an opportunity with his instrumental works, and some of the greatest of them he never heard at all. Only at an actual performance is a composer able to obtain an impression of his music from the necessary distance and judge its effect. And only this experience will enable him to assess critically what he has achieved and where he may have failed, quite apart from a factor which kept Brahms, to mention just one example, from ever having an orchestral work printed without having previously heard it: the possibility of misjudgment in assessing the balance of sound in a score can never be excluded. Live sound is always the most reliable argument and it is indispensable for even the most experienced composer. A case illustrating this will be discussed later.

It was Schumann who, speaking of the Great Symphony in C major by Schubert, coined the expression "heavenly length". This is the enthusiast's name for a peculiarity of Schubert's idiom which has never ceased to provoke annoyed opposition. In general, a feeling of length is attributable to vagueness, to a lack of precision. With Schubert the case is different: what appears as length comes from a superabundance of ideas, from the greatness of a conception that demands the corresponding space. And it comes from his nature, from the enthusiastic way in which he seizes his material, and never tires of enjoying again and again the magnificent visions he has created. In this respect, too, the experience he did not live to acquire would have had a moderating, cooling effect. All this does not alter the fact that his mature instrumental creations have a right to stand alongside Beethoven's as achievements of the greatest importance and originality, and that all those com- posers who came directly after him seem like pygmies beside a giant. Schubert was the only successor of Beethoven who could meet him at the same level, with a vision of the same cosmic amplitude.

The contrast between them is that of will-power as opposed to imagination, between an energetic, assertive nature on the one hand, and a pensive, contemplative nature on the other. It is obvious how decisive this disposition was for Schubert's destiny. It explains his lack of resistance, his incapacity to assert himself in life with the necessary robustness. And it was equally decisive for his art. The contrast between their characters is mirrored, as in a drop of water, in a minute detail of their style. Beethoven's most frequent expression mark, to be found on every page of his music, is *sforzato*, a sharp accent. Schubert's most frequent dynamic indication—one only needs to look at the music examples in this book—is *pianissimo*. Beethoven's form, the form of the man of will, could never be his. Therefore it does not make sense to measure his ideal of form against Beethoven's. The example of his great contemporary could strengthen him and help him on his way, but his instinct directed him towards different solutions, which were better suited to his character.

If we wish to study the specific features of his instrumental style, we shall have to concentrate on momentous individual cases in order to arrive at a kind of morphology of his work, as we did with the *lied*. It is in the nature of a fully-developed sonata form that it demands a strongly-defined main subject, distinguished by vitality of rhythm and motif, such as befits the hero, as it were, of the events. There are examples of this in every one of Beethoven's symphonies. Such a subject is marked by energetic articulation and a clear, sharply delineated succession of intervals. The hero stands before us as a personality; just as in a drama he has to prove himself by his actions, so, in a symphonic context, he has to show his mettle by developing thematic potentialities.

This principle is the basis of the vital tension of the form, and there are cases where Schubert completely adheres to it. Examples are the first movements of the Unfinished Symphony, the String Quartet in D minor, the Piano Sonata in D major and the Piano Trio in B flat major. But as a rule Schubert's opening subject has no inclination to behave like a hero. It has the dreaminess of a song tune, as in the "Trout" Quintet, the String Quartet in A minor, the String Quintet and the Piano Sonata—his last—in B flat; or, even when it leaves nothing to be desired in its rhythmical vigour, as in the late Piano Sonatas in C minor and A major, or the Piano Trio in E flat major, it seems unwilling to embark upon any conflict. Such a main subject, whose heroic attitude appears thoroughly convincing, makes its impressive entry, but very soon disappears from the scene and is not heard any more till, with the beginning of the recapitulation, all complications have been resolved and the succession of events can again take its course without further impediment.

Behind this odd contradiction of an unquestioned formal principle lies Schubert's instinctive reluctance to have his main invention, the fundamental fact of the composition in which his total feeling is anchored, pulled to pieces, as it were, by exposing it to the hazards of a development. This is repugnant to him, and so he prefers to gain the necessary material for a thematic development by making subordinate ideas productive, taking advantage of scraps of invention that have come into his hands as if by accident and whose potentialities no-one could have foreseen. In this more improvisatory than thematically constructive way all the demands of a richly conceived exposition and an effective contrast between this and a tonally restless, adventurously modulating development can be met.

The first movements of the two "posthumous" Piano Sonatas in A major and B flat major, the one of an energetic, the other of a lyrical character, are splendid examples of this standard type of Schubert sonata form. The opening subject of the great A major Sonata, with its strong and powerful shape, would honour any symphony, and one must understand what such a beginning means with Schubert: "Far, high, glorious"—this is a mountain top, an exalted sphere, to which only he can ascend:

This theme appears for a second time, even more strikingly coloured by the addition of an energetically superimposed descant. But after this it disappears and will not be encountered again until the beginning of the recapitulation. Yet the magnificent open view suggested by the theme remains, and everything that follows flows from an inspiration that dwells at such heights. And then comes a second subject, a genuine song tune, quiet and dreamy:

With Schubert such a beautiful thought is always spun out more extensively than a concise form would permit; it grows into an episode that occupies more than half of the exposition. When at length the initial phrase of the melody returns once more, as if for a last loving glance, the third and fourth bars are trimmed with a tiny ornament to which one might at first hardly pay any attention:

Here, however, there occurs a true Schubertian paradox: out of that chance ornamental motif grows a large, colourful development which does not require any further material. The composer begins to improvise on it and forms new inventions from the minute nucleus which has, after all, been no more than a cue for his creative imagination:

The second of these inventions runs directly into a carefully prepared, broadly-shaped transition, and when this at last leads to the reappearance of the grand main subject that we have not heard for such a long time, the circle of events is satisfactorily closed. The following recapitulation needs nothing else than the return of what has been heard before, with the obligatory transposition. Here, however, the composer has kept something up his sleeve, an effect as unexpected, if one considers the original character of the main subject, as was the improvisation in the development. That main theme re-enters in a coda, a postscript, but it has become tender, with a pensive conclusion that dies away *pianissimo*:

There is no doubt that this is church style. The suspended cadences in the fourth and ninth bars are unmistakable.

It is impossible to pass over this point without touching on a subject which is as important as it is difficult to grasp in rational terms: Schubert's peculiar relationship to a landscape, to an open-air background which, though it can be felt everywhere, defies exact definition. It is a peculiarity of his art that with him every experience wells up to direct expression, whereas with others it is filtered through deep layers and only becomes apparent in the work of art in a thoroughly sublimated form. Schubert is like a clear mirror. What he sees, what he feels, is directly reflected in his music, and this is perhaps the profoundest secret of his irresistible appeal. The distance from the impression to its artistic distillation is evidently shorter with him than, say, with Haydn, Mozart or Beethoven, with whom we hardly ever sense a direct reflection of nature. Again it is the exception that proves the rule, the exception being Beethoven's Pastoral Symphony. There is a fundamental difference between Schubert's spontaneous, unconscious reaction and a deliberate rendering of external impressions. Beethoven's remark "More an expression of feeling than painting" shows that the composer was aware of the questionable nature of an attempt to reproduce external impressions in music. Beethoven's landscape is conceived by a conscious intellect; it is seen "sentimentally", in Schiller's sense of the word. Nature, ever present in Schubert's music because he could not but reflect what filled him so overpoweringly, is felt purely intuitively, "naïvely" in Schiller's sense.

Here we come upon a peculiar feature of the Austrian landscape which Schumann, the sensitive observer, felt and described with such immediacy: it is "overlaid with a faint Catholic fragrance of incense". Everywhere in the Austrian countryside the traveller finds places of devotion: crucifixes, wayside shrines, memorial plaques commemorating a fatal accident, chapels by the roadside or at a cross-roads, or a *Waldandacht*, a place for prayer at a clearing in the woods, with pictures of saints attached to the trees and a few pews. Here, in the alpine air of this sonata movement, one might imagine such a *Waldandacht*, the expression of an unaffected, not in the least ostentatious piety, such as is so beautifully and spontaneously revealed in

Schubert's masses. Such episodes are not rare in his music. The sublimest of them, unequalled anywhere else, even by Schubert himself, is the deeply serious, solemn trio in the gay hunting scherzo of his String Quintet, and here his kinship with a late successor, Bruckner, is unmistakable; he shares Schubert's closeness to the Austrian landscape and in some respects seems altogether a kindred spirit.

The idea, then, of the background being mirrored in the music can be taken literally in Schubert's case, and this is presumably because the translation of feelings into musical terms was something which he had grown up with as a song-writer. A poetic image is a powerful stimulus for a musician with a lively imagination. This is true of Schubert, as, for instance, of Wagner. Inspirations such as the preludes to *Lohengrin* or *Tristan* would be unthinkable without their poetic background, and this is the only valid justification for music conceived from a "programme", from extra-musical ideas. As already mentioned, we can hardly speak of anything of this kind in Schubert's instrumental music. But he had formed his idiom as a tone poet in his early masterpieces of the *lied*, and the imagery of this language also lent its deep and colourful background to his instrumental music.

The musical equivalent of colour is harmony. If, with this in mind, we examine songs by Schubert which have an extensive poetic background—"Gruppe aus dem Tartarus", "An Schwager Kronos", "Ganymed" spring to mind—the first thing that strikes us is their extraordinary range of tonality. Schubert was the first to go beyond Beethoven in discovering harmonic possibilities of chromatic and enharmonic relationships which were to become of momentous importance in the further development of nineteenth century music. His treatment of harmony would deserve a special study. The interplay of major and minor, which has already been touched on, chromatically changed mediants, fancifully roving enharmonic changes are all means of colour which, in his thoroughly practical and completely uncontrived way, he explored in depth and integrated into his style. Even what Beethoven liked to call "the cobbler's patch"—a chromatically rising and modulating sequence, tabooed by theorists—is already to be found in "Gretchen am Spinnrade" and is an integral part of Schubert's

harmonic idiom; it is so indispensibly built into the tonal
context that nothing can be felt of the haphazardness that has
rightly discredited this kind of mannerism. Just to give an
example of a harmonic sequence which displays an extraordinarily colourful palette, including the richest variety of
chromatic twists, the tender epilogue to the second subject of
his String Quartet Movement in C minor may be quoted, one
of his numerous fragments and dating from a comparatively
early time (1820). At this point the dominant key, G major,
has been reached:

The unlimited breadth of the tonal horizon appears like a
symbol of infinity. Over and over again in Schubert's music
one meets that feeling of "Far, high, glorious", a pantheistic
view of the visible world as a manifestation of the eternal—
"God in Nature". This is the title of a wonderfully poetic piece
by Schubert which, like so many others, does not fit into our
standardised programmes and therefore belongs to the forgotten things. It is a chorus for female voices with piano
accompaniment, written for an enthusiastic singer and singing
teacher, Josefine Fröhlich, the sister of Grillparzer's "eternal
bride", Katharina. It is to Schubert's friendship with the
sisters that we owe two other glorious choral compositions of
his late period, written to poems by Grillparzer. In the piece
mentioned, there is a breathtaking moment of rapturous expressiveness:

"The dawn is but a reflection of the hem of His garment".

This is an apprehension of the eternal in lyrical contemplation, such as prevails in the first movement of the great Piano
Sonata in B flat, Schubert's last. The main subject is a true
song melody:

Such lyrical main subjects are also occasionally found with Beethoven, for instance in the first movements of the "Archduke" Trio, the 'Cello Sonata in A major, or the first Rasumovsky Quartet, and he could always discover symphonic potentialities in a lyrical invention of this kind. Similar things are even more frequent with Brahms, as in his Second Symphony, his two String Sextets or his three Violin Sonatas. With Schubert a song-like first subject will always remain within its original sphere of expression. It sings its way through to its heart's content, but shows no inclination to behave symphonically. The theme quoted above is no exception, and what follows as a second subject is no less lyrical, although it enters with a dramatic change of key to F sharp minor—this is a case of an enharmonically interpreted relationship to the submediant. Only in the codetta (the concluding section of the exposition) does a livelier mood come on the scene. It is necessary to have a closer look at this codetta motif which seems to be nothing but an arpeggio passage:

At the opening of the development a brief reminiscence of the initial melody, changed to the minor, makes its appearance. Then the third bar of this arpeggio passage re-enters, with a slightly altered accompaniment:

The left hand part can hardly be called a motif. It is nothing but a supporting bass, supplying the harmony. But out of these three notes the whole development section is to grow. Give Schubert three notes and on them he will improvise melody after melody:

In the context of a sonata development this is extremely unorthodox and would not be acceptable as a norm. For Schubert, however, it was the natural way of inventing and building, and he rarely departed from it. Melody remains for him the supreme truth; wherever he finds it he makes it welcome.

It may be necessary to explain the fundamental difference between the classical working out of thematic material and an improvisation like the one mentioned here. Thematic development obeys the conditions imposed by motivic relationships, just as in prose one thought follows another and every word has its place in the logical and grammatical context. In improvisation chance relationships prevail, as when trains of thought, led by chance associations, wander idly in all directions. To put it more concretely: improvisation is to thematic construction as a meadow is to a ploughed field, or after-dinner conversation to a lecture. The improviser uses the motif as a chance suggestion and roams freely beyond it into unbounded regions which have only a remote connection with the original subject.

In one particular case Schubert utilised this method consciously. His "Wanderer" Fantasy for piano is an improvisation on a *lied* melody. It follows a procedure frequently practised during the classical period: free improvisation on a given theme. At a time when this was a part of what an audience expected of a virtuoso, Mozart and Beethoven frequently improvised in public, and Mozart's pupil Johann Nepomuk Hummel, one of the most distinguished pianists and composers of the Beethoven era, had a great reputation as an improviser. The custom has been maintained longest among organists, whose practical duties in the church demand a certain skill in improvising. If one wanted to test the proficiency of an improviser, one gave him a theme, in order to judge his imagination and virtuosity by the way he treated this raw material.

This, then, is what Schubert does in one of his most outstanding piano works. The theme which he set himself was the nostalgic melody of the "Wanderer" (*"Die Sonne dünkt mich hier so kalt"*: "The sun that shines here seems so cold"). He treated it in the form to which he was accustomed, the sonata, linking its four movements by transitions. The song tune itself, the heart of the whole composition, is reserved for the second movement, adagio, where it appears for the first time in its entirety and is subsequently developed and varied in free style. In complete contrast to the "Trout" Quintet and the String Quartet in D minor, "Death and the Maiden", the emotional world of the song, from which the work has grown, remains restricted to this episode.

An essential criterion for free improvisation is its diversity. The composer has deliberately extracted the most varied possibilities and moods from a single motivic cell that the melody appeared to offer him, the dactyl in the first half-bar, and this dominates the whole spacious work from beginning to end.

This dactyl, consisting of a crotchet and two quavers, is one of Schubert's favourite rhythms. It is quite possible that it came from the unforgettable impression of the *allegretto* in Beethoven's Seventh Symphony, which, it would appear, had an incomparably fascinating effect on the contemporary public. Schubert opens the first movement with a spirited *allegro* version of this three-note motif, and he brings it to a cadence with a chromatic passing note, another motif that will gain thematic importance in the course of events. If, incidentally, one is frequently tempted in the case of Schubert to think in terms of verse metre, the reason is that Schubert's melody has its roots in a vocal imagination, so that in his instrumental music, too, one often seems to hear something like a verse rhythm—in this case the dactyl:

To this he opposes a second subject, an expressive, lyrical transformation of the dactylic motif, letting the chromatic passing-note grow into a little melodic appendix (a):

And, just as in the two sonatas which we have looked at, he uses this appendix to form a delightful new melody as an episode in the development. This passage is an invaluable demonstration of how melody can grow out of the most unlikely scrap of invention:

Thus one improvisation leads to another. In the scherzo the dactyl of the opening theme is changed into triple time, with a dotted rhythm. The old motif is easily recognisable in this disguise:

As so often happens in Schubert's scherzos, a waltz tune emerges. And in the trio we again meet the enchanting development episode from the first movement, now appearing masked in three-four time:

But now the improviser grows impatient. He shortens the recapitulation of the scherzo and storms through to the finale with cascades of passage work. Here the dactyl makes another return, this time in the guise of a ponderous fugal subject that introduces itself ceremoniously; it was part of the old tradition of extemporising upon a given theme that the improviser had to prove his contrapuntal mettle:

However, strict fugal style does not persist for long. Now the virtuoso comes into his own, and the conclusion is an outburst of pianistic brilliance such as cannot be found anywhere else in Schubert.

From all we know, he must have been a skilful though hardly a virtuoso pianist. His friends praise the sensitivity and colourfulness of his playing, especially when accompanying his songs. His pianistic style is demanding enough, even sometimes in his songs. But it hardly goes beyond Beethoven in the exploration of technical possibilities, and would seem to have been determined by the light touch and bright tone of the Viennese instrument of his period. The fuller, more sonorous possibilities of the English mechanism, of which, not long afterwards, Chopin, Schumann and Liszt were to make use, were evidently unknown to him. What most of all distinguishes him from Beethoven is the warm sensuousness of sound which, as in all his music, is also conspicuous in his piano style; this holds true of the sonatas discussed before as of the "Wanderer" Fantasy, where the veiled darkness of the adagio (see ex. 28) is extremely typical of his piano sound. Classical style avoids on principle such thick layers of chords where overlapping harmonics are liable to soften and blur the clarity of the harmony. Schubert was in fact a pioneer of romantic sound, and this is a characteristic of his piano style as it is of his chamber music and orchestral writing. A negative feature of this style is unmistakable: its lack of contrapuntal texture. Counterpoint is a sobering element, as its dependence upon a clearly articulated interplay of individual parts makes it intolerant of a superabundance of sound.

The positive aspects of romantic sound are less easy to define. Its most significant characteristic is the predominance of a smooth surface of rich sonority over sharpness of contour, of blurred dreaminess over clearly defined reality. The pedal, which had become an integral part of the piano mechanism in the early part of the century, would seem excellently suited for a demonstration of romantic sound, with all its virtues and dangers. It certainly plays an appreciable part in the development of romantic orchestral style. One of the peculiarities of the latter is a melodically leading, richly padded inner part, overlaid with a soft cushion of brightly coloured, intimately blending harmonic parts. The 'cello or the horn as tenor instruments are ideally suited to this situation.

In the first movement of the Great C major Symphony Schubert even uses three trombones in unison in an episode of mysterious grandeur; a call from another world intrudes on the bright, serene scene of the first movement. A flat minor, a key from the opposite end of the tonal spectrum, is a symbol of the distance. Such an invention all but bursts the narrow confines of the form. One could cut the whole episode from bar 174 to bar 240 without altering a single note, and no gap would be noticeable. It would only cripple the movement by removing its most beautiful episode. The marvel is that this intrusion from another emotional sphere springs from an instinct more deeply rooted than the conventions of form. The second subject of this movement, in contrast to the first, is not lyrical, as Schubert usually likes it to be, but rather capricious. It is as if it had caught a whiff of the nearby borderland, of Hungarian rhythm and melody which have left such noticeable marks in the following *andante*. The broad, wooded background of the introduction to the first movement, the most spacious pedestal on which a symphony has ever been put, seems to demand in the allegro a counterweight of a deeper, more expressive character, and this, in a higher sense, is the function of the mysterious episode:

This warm, sumptuous sound is something new in music. It belongs to Schubert in the same way as his fervently expressive melody, and cannot be separated from it. Gretchen's ecstasy, the Erlkönig's seductive whispering, the overflowing love of "Sei mir gegrüsst" are rooted in this sound. And Schubert's orchestral style is noticeably influenced by the song-writer's habit of shaping the accompaniment of a singing melody as a harmonically supporting ensemble of parts. If one regards the orchestra as enlarged chamber music, every part is a member of a community, having its own individual will and life, and this is true of Haydn and Mozart's orchestra, and in principle still of Beethoven's. With romantic sound, however, it can happen that the player is deprived of his individual identity by being subordinated to an effect of which he is not directly conscious. It was this that led to a rebellion of the orchestra when Mendelssohn tried to perform Schubert's Great Symphony in London. The place where this happened, in the last movement, is still a trial of patience for the first violins, who have to play a stereotyped, very tiring accompanying figure for eighty-eight bars:

Anyone who has ever heard this will remember the comfortably sauntering tune that sounds as though the singer could never again have any worries or sorrows, a tune to cheer even the most melancholy.

But this surely applies to the whole work; its richness explains why the author was unable to restrict its size, and why it has become customary to call it "the Great". It sounds like a paradox to state that its monumentality lies in the quiet repose with which one great panorama after another is spread out before us, a universe in sound such as has never appeared before or since. When, by way of comparison, one thinks of the depths and heights of Beethoven's Ninth Symphony, written a few years earlier, one arrives at a better understanding than words could transmit of the unbridgeable gulf between these two contemporaries. That Schubert, in all innocence, could set against Beethoven's epic and heroic ideal his own, directly opposed view of life, a quiet serenity unclouded by the stresses of will, was his greatest, though never fully appreciated, deed; in their opposition they are symbols of Schopenhauer's two basic forces, will and imagination.

Even here, true to his nature, Schubert remained an improviser; he himself has revealed how. In the autograph of the full score, there is a correction in the first movement so surprising as to surpass in curiosity anything else to be found in a work of genius pointing to its genesis. After finishing the full score he made an alteration at the beginning of the *allegro*, changing two notes that appear three times at intervals of two bars. With this correction he transformed a characterless formula into a pregnant, truly symphonic motif, worthy of the occasion; but this only as an afterthought!

It has been observed earlier that Schubert was capable of being satisfied with an insignificant opening, confident that in due course something different and better was sure to follow. Here he has excelled himself in this respect; he has succeeded in writing a movement of the most magnificent abundance. He started the *allegro* with a little nothing; but he became aware of this, and it disturbed him. His conscience warned him: something like this cannot be left as it is! The extraordinary thing is that the necessary surgery could be applied simply and locally. No further corrections became necessary; all he had to do was to perform the same little operation in a few corresponding bars at the end of the exposition, at the beginning of the development, and at the re-entry of the main subject in the recapitulation—which shows that he could make a significant alteration to the opening motif of an already completed large symphonic movement without further affecting the structure of the composition. But here we are back at the paradox of improvisation. The main idea which forms the nucleus of the composition and from which it grew is not at all the actual shaped motif but merely its dotted rhythm, the trochee, which, having already made a meaningful appearance in the second and third bars of the spacious *andante* introduction, proves itself, like the dactyl in the "Wanderer" Fantasy, to be a germ cell of inexhaustible fecundity.

It is curious to imagine the composer reading through his completed score, feeling uncomfortable because of a commonplace that had remained, then having a splendid idea of how to remedy this, and finding to his joy that it could be done merely by removing and substituting a few notes. It is a practical demonstration that the limits of symphonic style are less narrow than some preconceived ideas. Schubert is simply a unique case and must not be measured according to standard rules.

He never heard a performance of his greatest work. This explains some unsolved problems of interpretation, which are partly caused by the fact that its sound-perspective goes far beyond the range of the small-bodied orchestra to which he was accustomed. The attentive reader will not have missed an obvious problem of this kind in bars 5 and 9 of the main subject (ex. 37). Most probably he has never heard what is written

E

there, an expressive dotted motif in the top part continuing the throbbing triplets in the woodwind, a little phrase bridging the four-bar groups of the subject which would otherwise stand beside each other clumsily disconnected, and later culminating so beautifully in the melodious conclusion of the theme:

That such an essential detail remains practically inaudible in almost every performance, and that therefore an impression of squarely-built four-bar groups—tonic, dominant, tonic— prevails, is the result of miscalculated scoring. The composer has left these three notes, the continuation of the melody, to one oboe and one clarinet in octaves, and they totally disappear behind the strong entry of trumpets, timpani and strings in unison. If one wants to restore what the composer intended, even a drastic toning down of the unison entry will hardly be sufficient. One will have to strengthen the little phrase by additional woodwinds and perhaps even a horn. There are more places in this great work where without doubt the actual sound does not do full justice to what the composer had in mind, especially in the magnificently conceived trio section of the scherzo. In such cases nothing could be more con- venient and mindless than blind adherence to the letter. What matters is not the notes but what they signify, and this is as clear as the fact that the actual sound fails to do justice to it at such moments.

This mighty peak of Schubert's symphonic oeuvre has a counterpart in the crowning glory of his chamber music, the equally great String Quintet. Hardly more than half a year separates the two works. Apart from the key, C major, they share the wide horizon, the luxuriant sound and the over- powering impression of a landscape background. This is open-air music. In the scherzo, with its hunting fanfares and its solemnly devout trio, already referred to, the woodland background becomes quite unmistakable; and similarly in the *adagio*, the most extensive Schubert ever wrote. This melody flows under a starry night sky. But in the middle section an abrupt change of key occurs, from E major to F minor; it is again an enharmonic move, suggesting a dramatic change of feeling. It is as though the soul were torn by an unspeakable pain, a sorrow striving for expression, an inconsolable despair. A heart-rending phrase, repeated over and over again, seems to cry: "Why hast Thou forsaken me?" One cannot help remembering that this was written barely two months before Schubert's death, that he, with his alert instinct, must have sensed the danger that threatened him, and that the creative outburst of this year, with work following work in breathless succession, may have come from an imperative urge to rend from himself as much as possible of the tremendous visions which oppressed him with their profusion. Despite all the glory of this *adagio* it is difficult to bridge the gulf between two extremes of feeling when, after such an episode of despair, the return of the main key seems to restore the peace of the summer night with virtually no transition. The only unifying element, an agitated accompanying passage in the second 'cello, now develops, totally changed in character, into an ornamental background. But in the majestically rounded final cadence the intrusion of an F minor chord as a tragic reminder of the tormented episode is a deeply revealing feature of Schubert's language of the soul.

"Where others keep a diary in which they record their momentary feelings, Schubert confided his passing moods to music-paper; his soul, musical through and through, wrote notes where others resort to words." The young Schumann wrote this one year after Schubert's death. It shows how a close contemporary could already feel the element of spontaneous self-revelation in Schubert's music. The rarity of such unrestrained outbursts of suffering as the one mentioned above shows how alien the emotional exhibitionism of Romanticism was to Schubert. And his music tells us again and again of the youthful exuberance with which he was able to enjoy life.

Is it surprising that he prefers to tell us this in his native dialect? It breaks through with irresistible vigour and genuineness, not only in the more waltz-like scherzos but wherever a warm, good-humoured atmosphere prevails. One of its characteristics is a warbling high violin above an easy-going melody, the idealised traditional trio—violin, clarinet, and guitar—in

a wine tavern in the Viennese surroundings. For those who
know the idiom, there is nothing more attractive than just
this homely side of Schubert, Schubert himself, in his everyday
clothes. That his "everyday" touches the sublime is his greatness. This is where we find his Piano Sonata in D major. It is
fully part of the day-to-day Schubert. Anyone who wishes to
be happy for an hour need only sit down with it at the piano.
Here is the background of which Schumann wrote so enthus-
iastically, the town and its surroundings! There is nothing
richer in the sphere of sheer well-being, and no more credible
proof of the wonderful, ineradicable illusion that it is a joy to
be alive. An opening movement brimming over with vitality;
an *andante* that could only have been distilled from a dream
of wishes fulfilled; a scherzo full of the delicious freshness of
local colour, and not without a touch of tipsiness; and the
much-maligned finale, which crowns all. Philistines have
never been able to forgive the fact that this tune delighted
every Philistine when it was heard in "Lilac Time" of inglor-
ious memory. Schubert's marches for piano duet have deservedly
become popular; this is a march tune of the same kind, as
light-hearted as soldiers in peace-time. The relaxed way in
which this melody strolls along, the way the local Viennese
idiom turns pensive in a quieter episode and the march tune
finally dissolves in a rosy cloud of happiness, all this reflects
a day of undisturbed contentment.

But with Schubert there are so many of these, captured
in pictures which give every one of his late works its own,
unmistakable stamp. The Octet, the String Quartets in A
minor and G major, the two Piano Trios, the String Quintet—
every one of these great chamber music works has its own
specific colour, its own imagery. Each without exception betrays its relationship to the fountainhead of monumental
form, and each without exception transcends it, spreading
out its wings in a way which could endanger the integrity of
the form, were it not for Schubert's endless melody.

In the Octet, written in 1824 for a clarinet-playing patron,
Count Troyer, Schubert followed the example of Beethoven's
Septet in every external detail of its six movements, a form
stemming from the divertimento of Mozart's time, with a
scherzo instead of a second minuet and two quiet movements,

an *adagio* and an *andante* with variations. Schubert added no more than a second violin to Beethoven's ensemble, but how incredibly he has enriched the palette! This is by no means due only to the sound which, after all, is never more than a function of the substance; the colourfulness lies in the invention. Where Beethoven's Septet excels is in its crystal-clear form and perfect balance. This is still eighteenth-century music, music of the *ancien régime*. With Schubert the form has expanded into the blossoming regions of a romantic landscape whose delights are numberless.

A word must nevertheless be said about one of them: the conclusion of the *andante*, a set of variations on a fresh, spring-like melody, taken, as remarked earlier, from his singspiel *Die Freunde von Salamanca* of 1815. As is usual in his variations, the theme remains true to its original, cheerful character through-out, with a different group of instruments prominent in each case, just as in the variations in the Beethoven Septet. But after the last and liveliest seventh variation, when a short *più lento* epilogue follows, it is as though a cloud were casting its light shadow over the serene melody. A mood of pensive meditation descends. "God in Nature"! In Schubert's music it is only a step from cheerfulness to reflection, indeed even to melancholy.

The essence of such contemplative movements, idyllic calm, has no legitimate place in the dynamic context of a Beethoven-ian symphonic development. But even here Schubert manages to bridge the problem through the intensity of his melodic drive. In this, as already exemplified, he is liable to side-step the dramatic principle of the form, and yet succeed in achieving a satisfactory result in his own individual way. Interestingly enough, he could have justified his procedure with an example from Beethoven, in fact an isolated case of a very special kind, the first movement of the Pastoral Symphony. "Cheerful impressions received on arriving in the country": the peace and quiet of a summer landscape is symbolised by a pattern of form which intentionally avoids any dramatic climax, else-where of such importance to Beethoven. The development is shaped, as it were, in terraces. A thematic building-brick is used as an ostinato motif, growing into an idyllic episode of 46 bars. Having started in B flat major, it moves to G major (bars 151–96) and is repeated in an exact transposition (bars 197–242), now moving from G major to E major. There are thus two symmetrical planes which comprise almost the whole development of the movement. One can admire the form-instinct of the great architect who fulfils a particular task by for once completely ignoring his usual principles. With Beethoven this is a unique exception, responding to the demands of an idyllic concept; but in Schubert's music it can be found everywhere, because it is for him the most natural means of unrestrained invention. Almost the whole development in the first movement of his String Quintet—what follows is just a transition to the recapitulation—consists of an episode of thirty-six bars which, starting with an energetic contrapuntal phrase, soon flows into a broad song melody (bars 167–202), passing from F sharp minor to E major. This is immediately repeated, transposed one step lower (E minor to D major, bars 203–38). In the first movement of the Piano Trio in E flat he builds a large development episode of fifty-two bars, repeats it in exact transposition, then even starts the same episode a third time (the succession of keys is B major, F sharp major, D flat major), but after the thirty-second bar he makes it change its course into a transition, leading to the recapitulation.

The history of the evolution of form, as yet unwritten, is a fascinating subject. What theorists know about it hardly scratches the surface. The essential point is that experiments with form are hereditary; they are handed down to succeeding generations. Schubert's habit of forming development sections from symmetrical, terrace-like episodes was passed to Schumann, who was particularly fond of this method of construction. It is to be found, for instance, in his Piano Quintet, his First and Fourth Symphonies and his Piano Concerto. In the finale of the latter he even made use of Schubert's unconcerned method of starting a recapitulation on the subdominant in order to get through it without any alteration. In such matters Schumann was Schubert's most faithful follower. If with him the result is sometimes questionable, the reason is that his invention, however personal and appealing it may be, often remains confined to a mosaic of small musical tiles, thus giving a prevailing impression of an attractive miniature, unless a strong emotional impulse overcomes this. Schubert's method of building was simply not transferable. Its prerequisite was his long breadth, a greatness of conception transcending all narrow confines.

In one special case we can observe how his urge for expansive breadth has operated in the creative act itself. A full sketch has survived of the posthumous Sonata in C minor, the first of the three he wrote in September 1828, the year of his death. The sketch is complete in every detail as if it were a finished composition. Only towards the end does the composer seem to have had some doubts, but as a result he rewrote the whole work with many alterations which, especially in the last movement, are of momentous importance. The rondo subject, which, being based on a one-bar motif, was originally too short-winded, was expanded by a larger phrasing in four-bar groups, and this in turn gave rise to all sorts of other changes and additions in the course of a movement which in the sketch looks too brief and rather undernourished. A new episode in B major, a true riot of colour, has been unexpectedly improvised into it, and this raises the whole rondo to a higher sphere. Then, of course, there comes the long stretch of the Schubertian recapitulation, which we are familiar with and are usually happy to submit to. Here, however, there is somehow a feeling of going round in circles, of becoming bogged down. And when, after a beautifully poetic transition, the tarantella-like rondo theme makes its last entry, one misses the necessary final build-up. The composer no longer seems to be fully engaged. Perhaps a new invention has already seized his imagination and will not leave him in peace. Quickly—too quickly—he finishes the finale, and is already turning to yet another sonata.

6

DOMESTIC MUSIC

FOR MORE THAN a century music written for public performance has been virtually out of bounds for any but professional
musicians. The enormous increase in technical demands and
the discouraging effect of this on the would-be player have
resulted in a gap between the artist and his public such as has
never before existed in the history of music. In addition, the
ready availability of music through radio and gramophone
has undeniably contributed to making the amateur's efforts
seemingly futile. As a result, with an extraordinary standard
of virtuosity on the one hand and a steady decline in the
number of competent amateurs on the other, music has for
the vast majority become a matter of passive enjoyment. What
has been lost is the pleasure of doing it oneself, the delight
of a community of devotees for whom music-making is an act
of worship.

Such a problem did not exist at Schubert's time. Bach wrote
his music "for connoisseurs and amateurs"; and things were
not much different at the time of Haydn and Mozart, although
the range of public performance had widened. And Beethoven
began under practically the same conditions as his predecessors;
music not playable by amateurs would have been impossible
to publish. His first string quartets, Op. 18, were still technically
accessible to the good, experienced amateur players of his
time. But with the advantage of early fame he was able to
make greater demands, on players as well as on publishers.
His Rasumovsky Quartets of 1806, commissioned by a noble
patron for his excellent professional string quartet, go far
beyond such restrictions. And his last six string quartets, written between 1824 and 1826, are still among the most exacting
works of their kind.

Schubert, too, makes considerable technical demands in
his last, most mature chamber music. Beethoven's example
was a spur to his ambition, and his urge for an exuberant
display of sound likewise impelled him towards exploiting a

wider range of technical possibilities. But works in which this actually happened are exceptions rather than the rule, and the only ones of this kind for which he found publishers were the two Piano Trios Op. 99 and 100. Otherwise he nearly always wrote for "consumers", for music-loving amateur performers, from his early string quartets, which were played in his parental home, and the early symphonies, composed for his school orchestra, to the wonderful choral pieces of his last years, written for Josephine Fröhlich and her pupils. And musical amateurs were the customers on whom his publishers counted when, in addition to songs, they continually asked for smaller or larger piano pieces for two or four hands, dances of all sorts, or male voice quartets, a branch of choral music which was at that time beginning to be fashionable. In the list of works printed during Schubert's life-time, there is little else to be found.

Almost all his sacred music was composed for an immediate practical occasion, as for example his first Mass in F major, written for the performance celebrating the centenary of Lichtenthal parish church. It throws light on young Schubert's situation and on his remarkable diligence that on this occasion he wrote out all the choral and orchestral parts himself. Our present-day notions have to be completely discarded if we are to understand that it was worth any amount of labour to a composer to have the satisfaction of working for an immediate demand and hearing his music sung and played by people to whom it gave pleasure. Throughout his life Schubert wrote music for which he received no other reward, and material gain was the last thing he could expect. The nineteen-year old, who had since childhood devoted every minute he could spare to writing music, proudly entered in his diary on 17 July 1816: "Today I have for the first time composed music for money. Namely a cantata with a text by Dräxler for Professor Wattroth's name-day. The fee is 100 florins." This work, entitled *Prometheus*, a cantata for mixed choir and orchestra lasting three-quarters of an hour, was performed as a serenade on the name-day of a respected professor of law; very regrettably, it has disappeared without trace. According to contemporary reports it was a very impressive work. Schubert more than deserved his fee: as with the above-mentioned mass he was his own copyist, writing out all the choral and orchestral parts himself.

His creative impulse was never in need of strong incentives. When, after the first successful attempt to have works of his printed, publishers showed a certain interest in practical, easily marketable pieces, he had no hesitation in meeting such demands. The publishers' attitude to him can best be gathered from their letters; one must not forget that to them Schubert was a beginner who still had to prove his market value.

C. F. Peters, Leipzig, 12 November 1822:

. . . I am aiming at the works of artists who are already acknowledged, although I print some other things too. But if I receive enough from these, I must leave the introduction of new composers to other publishers; they can do something too. . . . But once a new composer has made his name and his works are recognised as good, then I am his man, for then the publication of his works accords with my purpose, which is based on honour rather than on gain; and I would rather obtain his works at a dearer price then, than have them cheaply at the beginning . . . .

Breitkopf & Härtel, Leipzig, 7 September 1826:

. . . As, however, we are as yet wholly unacquainted with the mercantile success of your compositions and are therefore unable to meet you with the offer of a fixed pecuniary remuneration (which a publisher can determine or concede only according to this success), we must leave it to you to decide whether, in order perhaps to bring about a lasting relationship by a trial, you will facilitate the matter for us and accept merely a number of copies in return for the first work, or works, that you send us. We do not doubt that you will consent to this. . . . In this case we propose that you should begin by forwarding us one or two pieces for the pianoforte, solo or duet. . . .

H. A. Probst, Leipzig, 26 August 1826:

. . . Selected songs, not too difficult piano compositions for two or four hands, agreeable and easily comprehensible, would seem to me suitable for the attainment of your purpose and my wishes. Once the path has been cleared, everything will find access, but to begin with, a few concessions must be made to the public. . . .

After his recital in Vienna in March 1828, Schubert, encouraged by the success of this venture, offered his Trio in E flat major to the publisher Probst in Leipzig, after having previously tried to interest Schott of Mainz. Probst quickly decided to acquire the work for a ridiculously small fee. Schott found a plausible excuse.

H. A. Probst, Leipzig, 15 April 1828:

. . . I accept, on your word, the Trio you have so kindly offered me, for a fee of 20 fl. 60 kr. But I still hope that you will shortly accede to my request to send me very soon some selected smaller things for voice or for four hands, a trio being as a rule only a prestige article and rarely capable of bringing in anything. . . .

B. Schott, Mainz, 28 April 1828:

. . . The Trio is probably long, and as we have recently published several trios, rather than do ourselves harm, we are obliged to postpone publication of this kind of composition until a little later, and you may feel this not to be to your advantage. . . .

This is not meant as an indictment of presumably responsible and well-meaning business-men, who operated with little capital in a market which was then only at the beginning of its development, but only as a demonstration of the immense difficulties against which a man of genius had to struggle in the 1820s. The question "How should a composer without the means of subsistence start his career?" would probably have elicited an answer in accordance with father Schubert's opinion: he should remain a schoolmaster and write his music on Sundays. As many a bad thing may still produce some good somewhere or other, one may assume that this cruellest

form of the struggle for existence may have had the result
that fewer untalented composers flourished than at a time when
the satisfaction of such ambitions demands fewer sacrifices.

There was, of course, a more direct way to break through to
success: via the operatic stage. The obscurity in which Schubert
lived and the weakness of his position with respect to publishers
can only be fully appreciated if one thinks of the many famous
contemporaries whom he saw before him (fully aware that
as an artist he towered high above them) and if one considers
the rude and unmistakable rebuffs he received whenever,
with inadequate means and inadequate support, he attempted
to intrude into the citadel where success and material security
seemed to beckon: the theatre. There is no need to think here
of the great men whose merits Schubert always acknowledged
with modesty and admiration, such as Beethoven, Weber, or
Rossini. But there was Spontini, Cherubini, Boieldieu, Auber,
Hérold, and Marschner; there was Spohr, whose *Jessonda* had
found a home in every German opera-house; there was Meyer-
beer, there was Donizetti, both with their first successful operas,
and in Vienna itself favourite composers such as Wenzel Müller,
Konradin Kreutzer, and Josef Weigl; and the latter, a composer
of popular shirt-sleeved operettas, had—as may be remembered
—been given preference over Schubert when, in 1826, the
position of deputy-conductor of the Court Chapel became
vacant. It is depressing to have brought home so forcibly
what a mirage fame can be, and how inadmissible it is to judge
an artist's importance by such an illusory criterion. But one can
understand why Schubert again and again tried his luck with
opera where more fortunate contemporaries, who could not
hold a candle to him, had apparently attained success without
difficulty.

Did he lack a gift for the stage? This cannot be asserted
categorically. Nobody would have dared to attribute this gift
to Beethoven, had he not happened to write a dramatic work
that will remain alive as long as there is an operatic stage. But
the fate of this work offers an important contribution to a study
of its composer's character. After the complete failure of
Leonore in 1805, he tried again, one year later, with an improved,
shortened version which met with no better luck. He did not
give in; eight years later, in 1814, came *Fidelio*, the final,

thoroughly revised version. This held its own and has become immortal.

It is equally characteristic of Schubert that he was never capable of taking a failure other than with resignation. Beethoven's iron will, the will to overcome any adversity or difficulty, of which every page of his sketch-books is documentary evidence, his determination to fight the angel—"I will not let thee go unless thou bless me"—was not granted to Schubert. If a work went badly, he dropped it. We shall have to deal later with this feature of his character in connection with one of his most outstanding creations. One must not imagine that for him to abandon in silence a work on which he had bestowed love and care can have been easy. No artist will relinquish a work without pain. But his richly blessed imagination enabled him to overcome such a failure soon enough. There were ever-new tasks for his creative energy. Shaking off the discomfort of his defeat, he would plunge headlong into a new venture.

A successful operatic composer would have had different opportunities. In the prevailing circumstances, Schubert's only chance was to produce music for domestic use, and to this we owe a vast number of compositions which he scattered abroad with lavish hand. If music were to be measured by the pleasure and happiness derived from it, Schubert's could claim first place. The superabundance we are offered nowadays in the theatre and the concert-hall, and with even less effort by radio, television and the gramophone, has almost made us forget the truism that there is only one direct approach to music: through the sacred activity of music-making. Once nobody would have doubted this; but it would appear that it has to be rediscovered today. Music-making is an act of devotion, the outpouring of a feeling which is infused with the purest, noblest essence of human love. Schiller cannot have been musical; otherwise he would not have forgotten joy in music in his "Ode to Joy". It is perhaps here that the deepest secret of Schubert's magic is to be found. Melody is a symbol of love. To sing it, play it, hear it or think it is for the soul to take a fresh breath. From melody streams the apostle's love without which man is but "sounding brass or a tinkling cymbal". In "Ganymed", one of his greatest songs, to words by Goethe,

Schubert has unburdened his heart of this feeling of all-embracing love. When, in a wonderful concluding phrase, the voice rises one step above the dominant—a typically Schubertian turn of melody—one feels the overflowing of emotion expressed in the simplest tone-symbol:

("Upward, towards Thy bosom,
All-loving Father!")

The blessing of this love is contained in even the most unassuming pieces he wrote for domestic enjoyment; it was his daily round to scatter such riches. He was always the giver, even at social occasions when he sat down at the piano and played waltzes for friends who wanted to dance. "Schubert himself never danced", writes Spaun, "and in fact he lacked physical agility in general." At that waltz-happy time there was always demand for dance music, and Schubert has left a hoard of such treasures. These dances became famous when Liszt transcribed them and played them with sensational success. The fees he received from Viennese publishers for his Schubert transcriptions were many times what Schubert had obtained for the originals ten years before; a famous virtuoso could make other demands than a poor composer.

During Schubert's lifetime, Josef Lanner and Johann Strauss the Father introduced the large waltz-suite in five parts with introduction and coda, which became the classical form of this type of composition. Normally, however, Schubert is satisfied with a loose succession of numerous short waltz tunes, usually consisting of two eight-bar sections—though it sometimes happens that an invention of a larger kind extends the form to twice this size or even more, and there are melodic, rhythmical and, most of all, harmonic subtleties which reveal the individuality of a great master amusing himself with trifles. He also used the same device of a sequence of barely connected short pieces for groups of Ecossaises, German Dances, Ländlers and Galops, always in an easy setting for piano and, just like Mozart's or Beethoven's German Dances, Country Dances and Ecossaises, intended for dancing. During the last years of Schubert's life, collections of dance music appeared, containing pieces by different composers, in which his name is to be found in close conjunction with the names of Lanner and Strauss, the popular founding fathers of the Viennese waltz. There is food for thought in the reflection that Beethoven made use of a simple tune taken from a group of twelve country dances not only in his ballet *Prometheus* but also in one of his most outstanding sets of piano variations, and that he finally put it on a throne of incomparable splendour in the finale of his Eroica Symphony. As can be gathered from this, there was as yet no barrier between dance and serious music—probably to the advantage of both.

Like the dance tune, the part-song belongs to the sphere of domestic music. It developed during the Renaissance period as the earliest manifestation of secular vocal art-music, gradually lost its popularity, and was practically extinct by the eighteenth century, with the exception of England, where its old tradition was never completely lost. In the course of the nineteenth century it became enormously widespread in the German-speaking countries with the development of the male-voice choir. As a composer of part-songs for male voices Schubert takes pride of place, a position uncontested to this day, though there was hardly a German composer of the nineteenth century who did not pay tribute to this humble branch of music.

Josef Haydn's brother Michael seems to have been the first to write male-voice quartets. But the acknowledged ancestor of this new species was Carl Friedrich Zelter who, in 1809, founded the first *Liedertafel* (Glee Club) in Berlin. As the name suggests, it was a sociable institution, an all-male party with drinking and singing; *Liedertafel*-style (as it was later called) deserves its dubious reputation. At Schubert's time there was already a considerable demand for part-songs of this type, which would also occasionally have been sung out of doors. This is evident in the fact that as well as an easy piano accompaniment Schubert wrote alternative guitar accompaniments for some of his male-voice quartets (incidentally this also applies to some of his songs). The Schubertians were no stay-at-homes, and music added zest to their amusements. It may be mentioned that even the piano, the all-purpose instrument, was sometimes used on excursions. In collections of old instruments one can see a *Wienerwald* piano from the Schubert period. It is not much bigger than an accordion, and could be carried on a shoulder-strap.

Schubert's part-songs for male voices—he wrote more than fifty—benefit from his early experience with all types of vocal music and his unequalled gift for poetic expressiveness. The male-voice song is limited to a maximum compass of two-and-a-half octaves. Schubert knew better than any of his successors how to achieve the utmost beauty of sound, plastic part-writing and expressive declamation within this narrow space, and, with the wisest restraint, kept within the vocal and musical limitations of untrained voices. He was the first great master of the male-voice choir and has remained its classic and patron saint. Part-songs such as "Der Goldelfahrer" (Mayrhofer), "Nachthelle" (Seidl), "Das Dörfchen" (Bürger) are distinguished by a melodic richness and poetic appeal found only with Schubert. And many of his choral composition owe their existence to chance occasions. What times these were, when a great poet like Grillparzer and a great musician like Schubert could join hands to write a serenade of incomparable poetic magic as a birthday treat for a fair lady! This "Ständchen" for contralto solo and male or female choir with piano accompaniment—each of the two versions has its own special beauty of sound—is one of the choicest pearls of Schubert's lyrical works for choir.

One of his works for male voices, however, has far outgrown the limits of what is usually to be found within this genre: *Gesang der Geister über den Wassern* (Song of the Spirits over the Waters), a large composition for eight male voices, accompanied by low string instruments, written in 1821 for a charity concert at the Kärntnertortheater. When he sets to music a Goethe poem of the great, transcendental kind, his spirit rises to hitherto untouched heights and finds new ways of expression and new subtleties of sound. For this occasion he had the required vocal and instrumental resources at his disposal. For its publication, however, this magnificent piece had to wait till thirty years after his death. It was, it is true, far beyond the capabilities of the *Liedertafel*.

A case such as this shows glaringly the limits of his freedom as an artist. Certainly, he was his own master, and no-one prevented him from writing what he liked. The only trouble was that there was nothing he could do with what he had written if it happened to lie outside the narrow restrictions which the iron law of demand imposed upon him. Fame alone could have helped him; and fame remained out of reach as long as he was confined to side-streets remote from the highways of publicity. To break out of this vicious circle would have required stronger elbows than his.

Thus he continued to be largely dependent on writing music which could bring him into direct contact with grateful consumers. One area of this kind with which he always kept his ties was church music, familiar to him from childhood. But here too he was inhibited in his freedom by practical considerations. Only one of his six masses found a willing publisher: the one in C major, written in 1816. This has an orchestral accompaniment for strings only; a group of wind instruments is added *ad libitum*, and can thus be used or omitted. Under the prevailing conditions in the church, a full orchestra, corresponding to the sound he desired, was available only on rare, special occasions. There is glorious music in these works, especially in his last two masses, in A flat major and E flat major, which, with those of Bruckner in D minor and F minor, can be regarded as the greatest settings of the mass after Beethoven. They appear all too rarely in concert performances, while today's demands for stricter orthodoxy concerning textual treatment have virtually excluded them from use in the church. Like many of his contemporaries, Schubert made cuts in the *Credo*, whose length poses problems of musical form. In his masses the words *credo in unam sanctam et apostolicam ecclesiam* are omitted. And in the Mass in E flat he so mutilated the sentence *Confiteor unum baptisma, in remissionem peccatorum, et expecto resurrectionem mortuorum* by contraction as to reduce it to nonsense. He had evidently forgotten the Latin he had learnt at school. No one has ever left such a quantity of precious music which, for one practical reason or another, has become all but inaccessible.

Should one also say this of the three-volume treasure of his piano duets, that inexhaustible source of pleasure and devotion for those rare music-lovers who today still cultivate this old-fashioned form of music-making? It would almost seem so. Until the beginning of our century the humble pastime of playing piano duets stood paramount in all domestic musical activity. At that time no major orchestral work was printed without the simultaneous publication of an arrangement for piano duet. This applied to the symphonies of Brahms and Bruckner as well as to the symphonic poems of Richard Strauss, Mahler's first four symphonies and the orchestral works of Reger and Debussy; it was the most obvious method of introducing a new work to the public. Then came a rapid decline in the desire for domestic music—which, to be sure, coincided with the emergence of an orchestral style that made the reduction of the sound to the black and white of the piano more and more problematical.

With regard to original composition for piano duet, just as with the *lied* and the male-voice part-song, Schubert can claim pride of place as both founder and foremost representative. For this combination, which first appeared during the last quarter of the eighteenth century, there are three exquisite sonatas by Mozart, as well as some stimulating compositions by Beethoven and Weber which also preceded those of Schubert. But none of his forerunners explored as he did the possibilities of sound and technique offered by four hands on a keyboard, and no one before or after him wrote works in the grand manner for this medium. He clearly enjoyed playing piano duets, as did Brahms, who became his most distinguished successor in this field, though without rising to the same heights.

This is indeed domestic music in the truest sense, music addressed not to listeners but to players, and even today, when practically all types of music tend to find their way to the concert platform, the piano duet is rarely performed in public. Nevertheless, even Schubert's sonatas for piano solo, which are by no means lacking in technical brilliance, had to wait almost a hundred years before virtuosos began to take a serious interest in them. Liszt adored them, but never included any of them in his concert repertoire, and the great pianists who came after him—Anton Rubinstein, d'Albert, Busoni, Paderewsky, Sauer, Godowsky—all fought shy of them. Evidently no one trusted their effectiveness with the public. One is astonished again and again at the length of time it took to recognise the greatness and nobility of music that appeals so directly to the hearts of players and listeners. Perhaps one day the same thing will happen with Schubert's piano duets, however little notice is taken of them today. That players love them above all else is, apart from the music itself, due not least to the comfort with which four hands can romp about freely on the keyboard, without ever getting in each other's way, or producing those thick couplings of sound that are otherwise one of the perils of this kind of setting, particularly in indifferent, mechanical arrangements. And the pleasure of joint music-making as an end and aim was always a rich source of inspiration for Schubert. Our world would be the poorer without these treasures, which are available to all those who will just take the trouble to reach for them with four hands.

It is difficult to choose favourites in view of the enormous variety. At the head stand the large works which demonstrate how Schubert's instinct for monumentality makes itself felt even under such unassuming conditions. Incidentally, one may also feel some respect for the technical demands that could be made on amateur pianists at that time. There are the wonderful Variations in A flat, dating from the summer of 1824, evidently written for the two young countesses in Zseliz. From the same period there is the Grand Duo in C major, which almost sounds like a symphony in disguise; Joseph Joachim actually orchestrated it. From the following year dates another duo, in E minor, on an equally grand scale. The publisher thought it too bulky, so it was divided into three separate pieces, *Divertissement* (Op. 63), *Andantino varié* and *Rondo brillant* (Op. 84, Nos. 1 and 2), which have remained thus separated to this day. (Something similar happened to the large piano sonata in G major, Op. 78; it was published as a set of four pieces, *Fantasy, Andante, Minuet* and *Allegretto*, and is still to be found like this in practically all editions.) There is the enchanting *Divertissement à l'Hongroise*, a further tribute to Schubert's aristocratic patrons at Zseliz, in which he comes to terms with the Hungarian idiom, as Haydn had done before, and Brahms after him. Schubert did not need to visit Hungary to become acquainted with this colourful style, since every Viennese must have been familiar with it from Gipsy bands in taverns and on the streets. There is a discreet reminiscence of it, as already mentioned, in the *andante* of the Great Symphony in C major, where an awareness of this picturesque background ought to prevent the conductor from taking too brisk a speed, which is, unfortunately, what he often does, and where the quiet clinking of spurs—an integral part of the Hungarian *csárdas*—in the martial counter-rhythm of the trumpet part at the beginning of the recapitulation should suffice to prevent any misunderstanding.

The crowning glory of Schubert's piano duets is probably the Fantasy in F minor, a treasure-trove in four interconnected movements. Here the designation "Fantasy" is justified by a very free formal lay-out, in which the finale is thematically linked with the first movement, and culminates in a vigorous fugato in triple counterpoint. It is altogether the most interesting episode of this kind in Schubert's music, and can be regarded as a symptom of his awakening interest in polyphony at this time. This work was a special homage to his pupil, the young Countess Caroline, to whom it is dedicated. It did not appear in print, however, until one year after his death.

There remain the many, many smaller piano duets, the rondos and variations, the marches and polonaises with their magnificently impulsive rhythms and their trio melodies, which flow from the fullness of a blest inspiration, melodies of which one can never tire, and which one might be tempted to call musical raw material: never has such precious substance been offered in such an unassuming form. The same could be said of Schubert's smaller piano solos, the two sets of four *Impromptus*, and the six *Moments Musicaux*. Such titles were invented by the publishers. Works of this kind were Schubert's answer to the constant demand for piano pieces of modest proportions and moderate technical requirements. But even there an over-anxious publisher was afraid that the key of G flat major might prove a deterrent to otherwise willing players, and published the *Impromptu* in question (Op. 90, no. 3) in G major, transposed one semitone higher. He evidently failed to understand that by doing this he not only impaired the sound, but even the ease with which it could be played; however, Schubert must have realised long before that there was no point in protesting against the arbitrary interference of publishers. Fortunately the original key has been restored in more recent editions, but this took a hundred years.

If here he had to take account of easy playability, in other cases, with a commission from a virtuoso, it was the opposite, the desire for brilliant technical display, that had to be satisfied. In the latter case, however, considerations of publication had to take second place. Schubert was always fond of treating one of his beloved song melodies instrumentally in a more elaborate fashion than was possible in the song itself, in order to exploit more fully the depth of its emotional content. The centre-piece of his extraordinarily brilliant Fantasy in C major for violin and piano, written for a virtuoso and a public perform-ance, is a set of variations on "Sei mir gegrüsst". And, to judge by the result, the variations he wrote on "Trockne Blumen", the eighteenth song of the cycle *Die schöne Müllerin*, must have been for a flute virtuoso of an equally high standard.

It is partly Schubert's own fault that the deep personal significance of this rarely played piece almost invariably remains misunderstood, and that the predominant impression is one of superficial brilliance, unless the two players—the piano accompaniment is as difficult as the flute part—are conscious of a quite different emotional world hidden behind the brilliant paraphernalia. It may also be felt as a contradiction that a set of variations leading to a climax of technical fireworks should be preceded by a deeply serious, totally introvert introduction, which cannot possibly be understood but in the closest connection with the tragedy of the young miller. One can feel the deepest emotional involvement in this introduction, a requiem without words for the ill-fated hero. One must not think of the sentimental poem but of what Schubert has made of it: the antithesis of an individual's tragic fate and eternal nature, engendering new life. Here again the contrast of minor and major tonality proves to be an obvious symbol. For one bent on death the thought of a new spring he will not live to see, and its splendour, is desperate consolation:

> Dann Blümlein alle, heraus, heraus!
> Der Mai ist kommen, der Winter ist aus.

> (Come out then, flowers, and bloom once more!
> May has come, the winter is o'er.)

Here Schubert finds the way to a pantheistic apotheosis, the triumph of eternal spring over all human futility. He ennobles everything he takes into his hands by the fervour of his emotion. The major key has already gained the upper hand with the phrase "May has come" in the penultimate variation. The last one, overcoming melancholy reminiscences, expands into a brilliant finale, a triumphal march for victorious nature, a song of rejoicing offered to the new spring. Once more it must be said that I have no wish to attribute to Schubert any descriptive intention. He never hides any secrets in his music. He follows an inescapable urge, which strives within him for expression. No poetical programme is needed because poetry is in his soul and flows into his music, through which it speaks irresistibly if the players themselves feel and communicate it. In this work, however, misunderstandings can easily occur. The questionable element of the virtuoso style, evidently occasioned by the external circumstances of a commission, stood in the way of the composer's expressive instinct. This has to some extent resulted in a hybrid, because poetry and outward brilliance are difficult to reconcile. The task can nevertheless be accomplished satisfactorily, but only if the necessary consideration is given to the expressive background, which presupposes a conscious understanding of the problem.

How even an enthusiastic Schubertian could innocently miss the point is demonstrated by Kreissle, who writes of this work: "Schubert here had the intention (and was probably not allowed to have any other) of offering the flautist and the pianist an opportunity to show their virtuosity on their respective instruments. Both are fully occupied with runs and figurations, and this work is only digestible nowadays when performed with great fluency as well as purity of intonation and precise co-ordination. As with almost all such occasional pieces, the composer has undoubtedly dashed it off in a hurry, without giving it any further thought."

In so many other cases, a rugged exterior impedes access to a work of art; with Schubert it is often a gentle, pleasing surface that conceals its profundity.

One thing should have become abundantly clear from this survey of Schubert's relationship to the consumers of his music: that the limitations imposed on his creative work by the narrow conditions of demand must often have been desperately irksome and frustrating to him. Comparisons with Bach, Haydn or Mozart break down because times had changed. The eighteenth-century composer could still accept his position as an artisan who carried out the task prescribed him, with the belief in a God-ordained world. In return he had his livelihood and his legitimate place in human society. Mozart, who felt this situation to be humiliating, rebelled against it and had to pay for this with lifelong insecurity, continually beset with debts. Beethoven, favoured by a new cultural climate as a result of the French Revolution, was able to maintain his independence and keep his aristocratic patrons in a state of salutary respect. Schubert was exposed to the economic conditions of the new century without any protection. He found himself in the trough between two crests of the wave; he was as dependent on commissions as his predecessors had been in the eighteenth century. But what he received for his work was a pittance, and an iron ring of mediocrities kept him from reaching the heights where he might have found freedom and material security.

It is necessary to understand these circumstances in order to appreciate how much idealism and renunciation a life's work such as his involved. "*And yet*" is the invisible motto at the head of all he created.

7

UNFINISHED WORKS[1]

A NECESSARY COMPLEMENT to the creative impulse is the will to finish the work. Were it not so, there would be a thousand unfinished masterpieces, for no important work has ever come into the world without difficulties of one sort or another, internal or external obstacles, or problems of shaping that had to be overcome in order to bring to realisation the ideal image in the creator's mind. This demands the involvement of the whole personality and a strength of will steeled by experience. The work itself rarely betrays any sign of this struggle. Occasionally one learns of it through the history of its genesis, occasionally through sketches and the clues they give us to the difficulties encountered in shaping an idea, as particularly in the case of Beethoven, who sketched extensively. The will to conquer, to finish his work, is the artist's categorical imperative. Death alone can defeat it. Those musical masterpieces that have come down to us as fragments—Bach's *Art of Fugue*, Mozart's *Requiem*, Bruckner's Ninth Symphony—bear witness to this fight to the last breath. Death has set its seal on these works.

There is one exception. Schubert's Symphony in B minor is the only great work that a composer has laid aside unfinished without any apparent external compulsion.

A lot of printer's ink has been spilt over the question as to why the B minor Symphony has remained a fragment. It was an act of touching naïvety to offer a prize for its completion on the occasion of the hundredth anniversary of Schubert's death; and still more naïvety was needed to compete for the prize. First of all, we must consider the history of this work; it is curious enough, and symptomatic of the fate of Schubert and his artistic legacy.

The symphony as we know it was sketched in October 1822,

---

[1] In this chapter use has been made of an article by the author, published in *The Music Review*, Cambridge, 1941/I.

and Schubert started to write the full score on the 30th of this month, as the date added to it indicates. As usual, he must have worked in frantic haste, for in November, after completing the two known movements of the symphony and roughly sketching a scherzo to follow them, he was able to lay them all aside and finish another large work, the Wanderer Fantasy. In the following spring, at the instigation of his friend and admirer Johann Baptist Jenger, Schubert was awarded the title and diploma of Honorary Member of the Styrian Music Society in Graz, and in his letter of thanks Schubert promised the Society to show his gratitude by dedicating a symphony to them, perhaps with the one in B minor in mind. In September of the same year, 1823, he handed the score to his friend Josef Hüttenbrenner, who was to take it to his brother Anselm, a member of the said Society. In actual fact, Josef only took the manuscript to Graz four years later, in 1827. Anselm received it and kept it instead of handing it over to the Society, and it appears that Schubert took no further interest in it. Anselm owned other Schubert manuscripts, among them the operas *Des Teufels Lustschloss* and *Claudine von Villabella*. Parts of the latter were once used for lighting a fire, and were thus lost for ever, but this was only due to negligence.

It must be added that the brothers Hüttenbrenner belonged to the inner circle of Schubert's friends. Anselm, a composer and respectable pianist, was Vogl's accompanist when, in 1821, the latter gave the first public performance of Schubert's "Erlkönig", at a charity concert at the Kärntnertortheater. At that time the brothers did their utmost to further their friend's fortunes. They seem to have appreciated the artistic value of the unfinished work of which Schubert never spoke and of whose existence neither his brother Ferdinand nor his friends ever knew. In any case, Josef uttered remarks to this effect when giving information to Schubert's biographer Kreissle, though this was many years later, towards 1850, when Schubert had become famous and Anselm had been forgotten. It was also through Josef that Johann Herbeck, who conducted the concerts of the Society of Friends of Music in Vienna, heard of the existence of the symphony, which stirred his curiosity. He went to Graz to see Anselm, and managed to coax the precious manuscript from the unsociable old crank by offering him a performance of one of his orchestral works in Vienna, a promise he faithfully kept. Half a year later, on 17 December 1865, forty-three years after it was written, Schubert's Unfinished Symphony had its first performance in Vienna. As the presentation of such a torso evidently seemed too odd, Herbeck added the finale of Schubert's youthful Third Symphony, in D major, to it. Similar scruples must have been felt in London when the Unfinished Symphony was performed there in 1867, for on this occasion the Entr'acte in B minor from *Rosamunde* was added, which may at least have been a little more suitable as a finale. The work, which, without exaggeration, may today claim to be the most popular symphony in existence, was published in 1866.

The behavior of Hüttenbrenner, who sat on this precious score for more than forty years, is strange, but it may perhaps be explained by an unsuccessful artist's unconfessed jealousy of the now famous friend whom he had once patronised. There are people who have a special gift for pushing themselves into the vicinity of the great, and whose ambition finds a certain satisfaction in the reflected glory that falls upon them. Anselm Hüttenbrenner seems to have been one of this brand. The fellow appears almost uncanny when one gathers from the biographies by Schindler and Thayer that he was the only witness of Beethoven's death and closed the deceased's eyes.

Forty years later the obtrusive busybody had become a peevish recluse. Even if one is inclined to interpret his conduct as the instinctive manifestation of an inferiority complex, there still remains the enigma of Schubert's behaviour; and this is the reason for all the puzzled conjectures that have always surrounded the Unfinished Symphony. The theory that the symphony was completed, but the second half lost, has proved untenable because it is refuted by the actual manuscript as well as by the circumstances that the composer continued to ignore a work of such importance, and that furthermore it was not even included in the list of works compiled by his brother Ferdinand after Schubert's death. The assumption that it was intended as a work in two movements, in two different keys, is too silly to be taken seriously; moreover, the existence of a sketched scherzo is visible evidence against this. It is clear, therefore, that there must have been inner reasons why the composer abandoned a work of such tremendous significance.

Strangely enough, no one has so far connected this question with a circumstance that has a strong bearing on the psychology of Schubert's creative activity. He left a striking number of unfinished works, more than any other great master, and these fragments tell a story which is worth following up, because, taken in conjunction with the existing sketches of the symphony in B minor, it yields a fairly unequivocal clue to what really happened.

When an artist abandons a work, there are two possible causes: he has arrived at a critical point where difficulties have emerged which are hard to resolve, or else he has recognised that the work he has begun suffers from fundamental defects that cannot be remedied. Sometimes the former reason has been brought about by the latter: at a decisive moment it turns out that the premises were faulty, that something has gone wrong with the material or with its shaping. It is evident that crises of this nature happen more often to a young artist who is still in the process of developing his technique than to a mature one who has become sure of his hand through long experience. But Beethoven's sketches tell us of all sorts of drafts begun and not completed, and it is known that Brahms, even at the time of his fullest maturity, rejected and destroyed one or another work he had started. It is obvious that something of this kind can always happen, but only rarely, and hardly ever without the most cogent reasons.

For a young composer who is still working at forming his hand, it is a very natural thing to get stuck, Schubert could already write masterpieces of the *lied* at the age of seventeen, but as far as instrumental music was concerned he was still a novice at twenty, in spite of a profusion of early works; and he had no one to advise him. As a boy he had gaily worked away, without scruples or inhibitions. The seventeen-year-old writes proudly under the first movement of his String Quartet in B flat major: "Written in $4\frac{1}{2}$ hours" (5 September 1814). Later on, with more fastidious claims, his self-criticism awoke. To work more slowly, more deliberately, was something he never learnt, but he did learn to be dissatisfied with what he had written so quickly, which is the true artist's first and most indispensible postulate. The composer of "Erlkönig" could no longer be satisfied with the comfortable platitudes which were still liable to flow from his pen when he was writing instrumental music. In February 1815 he started a piano sonata in E major, his first attempt of this kind, but he did not progress beyond the middle of the first movement. The beginning is amazingly indifferent: an ascending E major scale, and an ascending arpeggio on the dominant. He could hardly have got away with less. Later on, admittedly, some genuinely Schubertian features make their appearance and the exposition is tolerably rounded off. But the development section completely loses itself in aimless meanderings, and in the middle of a phrase he breaks off; one can see that the composer has lost heart. One week later he began another sonata in the same key, and this time managed to finish three movements, as far as a minuet, before he gave up, evidently dissatisfied with the whole business, and without any inclination to throw yet another movement, a finale, into the abortive venture.

More than a year later he started a piano sonata in F sharp minor whose opening looks very promising; but this again did not progress any further than the first, namely to the middle of the development section in the first movement, where he found himself entangled in difficulties; and there are half a dozen other sonata fragments from the following two years; they consist of completed or half-completed movements. When he had the feeling that the right impulse was absent, he gave up the struggle. He had no patience to wait for a better frame of mind. In all these cases one can surmise with fair accuracy what has happened. The momentum of the invention has carried him up to a certain point where he has stumbled, as it were, on to a wrong track. He now looks back, examines what he has written, notices some inadequacies, and loses his pleasure in the work. He starts something new in order to drive the miscarried piece from his mind, and lays it aside.

It is characteristic of his stage of development at that period that here and there such abortive attempts contain more original, more personal features than the symphonies written in the same years, his Fourth, Fifth and Sixth, in which he was clearly and all too noticeably following established classi-

cal models. Impersonal conventionality could still happen to
the twenty-year-old. The problem of finding his own, characteristic mode of expression and form could only be solved step
by step, and it is precisely in those places, where his own
specific, personal way of inventing asserts itself, and where
the inherited phraseology can therefore no longer be of any
use, that the difficulties of shaping increase. Well-meaning
editors who set out to complete such fragments fail to see the
elementary fact that the composer does not abandon a work
because he is unaware of the value of his invention, but because he has noticed certain shortcomings which are intolerable
to him, and whose elimination would involve turning the
whole composition upside down. If he is not in the mood to
undertake such an operation, he discards the work and puts
it into his drawer.

Brahms was more circumspect than Schubert. He destroyed
such sketches or fragments, and thus spared well-meaning
editors their trouble.

One circumstance that may explain a great deal was Schubert's habit of working in frantic haste. There is a testimony
to this haste which can claim to be a unique curiosity. It
consists of a double sheet of music-paper, containing on the
outer pages, 1 and 4, the original manuscript of one of Beethoven's best-known songs, "Ich liebe dich". Schubert, we
are told, received it as a gift from Anselm Hüttenbrenner who,
as previously remarked, had access to Beethoven. On the two
inner pages, 2 and 3, Schubert wrote a sketch of the *andante*
movement of his piano sonata in E flat major, Op. 122, up to
the beginning of the recapitulation. Below this there are some
scribbles: the composer was apparently demonstrating to a
pupil the mysteries of the treble and bass clefs, and there are
writing exercises underneath. One can see that Schubert
spared no thought for external matters when he was at work.
He happened to need a sheet of manuscript paper, and it
would obviously have taken too long to look at what was
written on the other side.

All this does not alter the fact that the propensity to give up
a work at the first sign of difficulty has its dubious side. As an
example of the opposite, one need only think of the twenty-
year-old Brahms, who carried his first great labour, the Piano

Concerto in D minor, around with him for five years, before being able to finish it to his satisfaction.

That Schubert yielded so easily to the temptation to evade such an effort can perhaps also be explained by a positive quality: his irresistible creative urge at this, the youthful spring-tide of his creative life. Nothing could help him so effectively out of the annoying embarrassment of having reached an impasse as the pleasurable sensation of an enticing new adventure for his imagination. And there was never any lack of such stimulation.

The "Trout" Quintet of 1819 proclaims for the first time the true master of instrumental music. This work, too, shows signs of haste in its form, which is in many ways schematic, as was pointed out earlier; but by now the style is firmly established, and thus a position has been reached from which compromises are no longer possible. A highly important work from the following year, the String Quartet Movement in C minor, has long found its legitimate place beside Schubert's three last and greatest string quartets. But how uncertain the conquered ground still was! This first quartet movement has remained a fragment just like the Symphony in B minor, and it is by no means free from certain questionable features in spite of its great beauty. The agitated tremolo motif that opens the movement and takes the place of a main subject is hardly more than a formula and its thematic function remains subordinate. The key, C minor, disappears after the first twenty-two bars and does not return until the very end, in the last eleven bars of the movement, forming a rather make-shift and unconvincing coda. All the same, it is a movement of the richest melodic invention and extraordinary colourfulness.

After this, Schubert started an *Andante* in A flat major, but did not continue it very far. This fragment was published in the editors' notes in the Complete Edition, and one can see that the same thing occured as with the sonata movements mentioned before: the composer ran into difficulties and abandoned the work. The beginning is genuine Schubert, imaginative and expressive, but it is built on a one-bar phrase, an invention not large enough in scope for proper development. This soon becomes apparent when the composer tries to expand the motif and does not really succeed in getting anywhere.

Perhaps he has become aware that he has landed in an exact quotation from Florestan's aria in *Fidelio*:

As if in annoyance at this, he turns away into fast figurations, first with semi-quaver triplets, then with demi-semi-quavers; he modulates aimlessly, and thus the composition finally falls to pieces. He puts the failure away and takes refuge in *Gesang der Geister über den Wassern*. When his imagination is stimulated by the poet's words, he feels that he is on safe ground.

It is significant that during the two years following the Quartet Movement Schubert was able to finish quite a number of his most outstanding *lieder*, but not a single instrumental composition. For a man with his immense productivity this must be taken as an unmistakeable indication of a problematical state. The "Wanderer" Fantasy, written towards the end of 1822, immediately after the interruption of his work on the Symphony in B minor, was the first composition to break this spell; but not until 1824, with the String Quartet in A minor and the Octet, did the unchecked flow of his great instrumental works begin. The riddle of the B minor Symphony can only be explained in the context of a persistent crisis in Schubert's instrumental writing.

The situation becomes even more unmistakable when one takes into account that the "Unfinished" had been preceded one year earlier by another unfinished symphony which, for several reasons, deserves some attention. Though not quite as bizarre as the story of the Symphony in B minor, that of its predecessor is not lacking in interest either.

In 1846 Mendelssohn received as a token of gratitude from Schubert's brother Ferdinand the manuscript of a symphony in four movements which Schubert had sketched in August 1821. Part of it—a slow introduction in E minor and 110 bars of a following allegro in E major—is finished in full score. The remainder of the four-movement work is a skeleton of a full score in which the whole thread of events is indicated, without interruption, by one or another melodically leading instrument.

Everything else is confined to an occasional fragment of accompaniment, a hint at a bass line, or an inner part to suggest the harmony. Paul Mendelssohn, who had inherited this manuscript from his brother Felix, presented it to the well-known Schubert scholar and enthusiast George Grove in London in 1868. A letter from Brahms to his friend Joseph Joachim, who was staying in London at the time, refers to this. Brahms only knew of the symphony by hearsay and assumed that it was one of Schubert's late works. But in such a case his own feelings were unequivocally against any attempt to intrude into the inaccessible realm of a sketch, especially as he knew from personal experience that a composer has sound reasons when he discards a composition, and that no one can dispute his right to decide what he considers worth making public. "I presume you know", he writes to Joachim (December 1868), "that Schubert's last symphony came via Ferdinand Schubert to Mendelssohn. The introduction and half the first movement are completed in full score. From then on the whole symphony is apparently sketched out, and in such a way that there are notes in every bar, a sight both lovely and sad, as I know from my acquaintance with *Sakuntala* [an operatic sketch by Schubert] and other things. This sketch has long been thought lost. Now Paul Mendelssohn has sent it to London to Mr Grove! This would have seemed to me hard to believe, had I not read it in a letter from Mr Grove himself. If at all possible, the symphony will now presumably be made usable post-haste for a performance. But can you, or will you not try, meanwhile, to lay a restraining hand on it?. . . Many may well feel a desire to fill in the score, say Costa or Benedict [popular conductors in London]. But if Mendelssohn did not have the courage to do it, and if you cannot find it either, when you have had a look at it, then please make sure that no indecency is perpetrated with it! In short, I feel you ought to try to obtain some rights over it. . . ."

It is not known whether Joachim took any action in this matter. But Brahms's apprehension that his own profound sense of reverence and responsibility towards such a relic was not to be expected from more thick-skinned people, less inhibited by expert knowledge, turned out to be justified. Grove could not resist the temptation of presenting the world with a new Schubert symphony. At his instigation John Francis Barnett, a renowned English composer, "filled in the score", and the work was performed in London in this version. A piano reduction of it was published in 1884; judging from this, one must admit that the editor fulfilled his task with reverence and a good sense of style. In 1934 Felix Weingartner published a new version of the score, unfortunately not without some crude errors in the part-writing and misconstrued harmonies. Since then the symphony has occasionally been performed in this version.

What interests us here is the quality of the original, and this is, to use Brahms's expressive term, "a sight both lovely and sad", for there are some beautiful things in it as well as much that is second-rate, above all many relapses into the immature style of Schubert's early symphonies and overtures, and this makes it understandable that he should have lost the desire to go on with it.

The method of starting a score by inserting only a few single instruments, leaving everything else open, looks somewhat bewildering to the present-day musician. This procedure was, however, not at all unusual at Schubert's time, and obviously had its roots in the figured bass method of the baroque period. Hummel relates that his teacher Mozart used to sketch in this way, and Adolf Bernhard Marx, who recommends the method in his manual of composition of 1847, quotes Hummel as follows: "It is no small advantage that with this method of writing the score grows fast and one can see something finished in a very short time, while by writing out one page after another in full one never seems to make any headway. Moreover this is of greater importance for the progress of the work than one would think. One is in good spirits and carries out one's task with greater ease and willingness. And in the long run, though it might seem to require more time to keep going back to the beginning again, the work in fact takes less time. Mozart could not have written so much without this method."

In this case it seems to have induced Schubert to work even more hurriedly, for the whole draft suffers from carelessness. The weakest part is probably the first allegro which worries to death a dotted rhythm and a humdrum motif, while the subsidiary subject looks lame because it cannot escape from one central recurring note, A. The only movement that rises to the full height of Schubertian invention, and whose loss one must sadly regret, is a tender *adagio* of simple design. The following scherzo would fit into any one of Schubert's early symphonies. And the finale bustles away without really getting anywhere; here too the thematic material lacks everything that pertains to Schubert's mature style. He may not have been able to suppress the feeling that he had done this sort of thing better before, or that he had not fared any better here than two years earlier with another, even poorer-looking symphony in D major, similarly abandoned as a sketch.

An unfortunate side-effect of the discovery of these symphonic miscarriages is that it has played havoc with the numbering of Schubert's symphonies. The Great Symphony in C major, which started its career as the Seventh, has in the meantime gradually advanced to No. 11, owing to those that have come in between. Apart from the "Unfinished" and the two above-mentioned sketches, a ghost symphony has crept in which was baptised "Gastein" or "Gmunden-Gastein" Symphony, and is assumed to date from 1825. Yet nothing more is known of its existence than remarks in some letters of Schubert's friends, saying that he was writing a symphony, or had finished writing one. Quite apart from the facts as such—a sketch is not a finished work, and a ghost still less—it is incomprehensible why numbers are not left alone, since their main purpose, that of identifying a given work, is rendered illusory if they are changed over and over again. Bruckner showed wise forethought when he called a symphony written between his First and Second his "Symphony No. Zero", having found it inadequate and laid it aside. Very reasonably it remained "No. O" when it was published in the Complete Edition.

But let us return to the work which has caused this whole digression, the torso which, as the "Unfinished Symphony", became, nearly forty years after the composer's death, one of his most widely appreciated works and a crown jewel of European music, but whose disappearance from the world without trace would never have been noticed, had the manu-script suffered the death by fire which, as mentioned earlier, had befallen another irreplaceable Schubert manuscript at

Anselm Hüttenbrenner's house. The work requires no commentary. The magnificence which Schubert has achieved here is due to the fact that, true to his nature, he was able to remain a lyricist from beginning to end, and yet could find the breadth of scope and the dramatic contrasts implied by the grand style of a symphony.

The juxtaposition of these two movements is in certain respects paradoxical. To obtain a different visual impression in the notation, Schubert's time signature for the *andante* is 3/8, as against the 3/4 of the first movement. This, however, does not alter the fact that the pulse of the two movements is practically identical, which anyone can test with the help of a metronome. This would be unthinkable with Beethoven, to whom a sharp contrast between two successive movements is axiomatic. Yet no-one could accuse the symphony of lack of contrasting effect, and this is because the lyricist has other means of confrontation at his disposal than a mechanical change of speed. As a matter of fact, these two movements have not only the same speed but also the same lay-out. They are both in sonata form; both culminate in strong development sections; and in both there is very much more *piano* than *forte*. Their contrast is based upon what I would call the degree of tension of the lyrical expression. And, as always with Schubert, the decisive factor is the structure of the melody. In the first, passionately tense movement, melody is like a dramatic dialogue, restless and agitated, alternating between low and high voices. In the *andante* it flows like a calm river, and the dramatic conflict is concentrated in a single episode. Both movements are without equal in Schubert's symphonic music, in their greatness of conception, impressive thematic beauty and richness of sound. And every conductor knows that there is no masterpiece whose performance is so unproblematical, simply because in this marvel of a score every note is unmistakably in its place.

This is an eruption no less momentous than "Gretchen am Spinnrade" had been eight years before. For the first time Schubert here realised his own ideal of the symphonic. In one burst of inspiration he wrote down something which placed him beside the dreaded, the adored Beethoven. And he left his work, this great vision of a new world, unfinished! Can one wonder that this has given rise to endless speculation? The essence of the matter is that in the absence of external factors that could offer an explanation, the reasons for something so erratic can only be found in the music itself and in the mentality of its author. Regarding the latter, we know of Schubert's fateful readiness to give up a work when difficulties arose. And what the music tells us about the mishap stands unambiguously in the draft of the scherzo that was to follow the first two movements. This draft also definitely refutes—as already mentioned—the altogether absurd assumption of a deliberate two-movement design.

When, fifty years ago, I revised the score for the Philharmonia Edition in Vienna, I added this sketch as a supplement, assuming that no further commentary was required. As it has turned out, this expectation was a piece of unjustifiable youthful optimism, and the debate about the riddle of the Unfinished Symphony has gone on. The sketch is reprinted here (see ex. 41). It consists of one page in full score, containing the first nine bars of the scherzo.[1] The whole scherzo and the first section of the following trio are sketched out. Like the existing sketches for the first and second movements of the symphony, the draft starts as a full piano reduction, containing all the details of the texture. After the first double bar, however, the setting becomes thinner, being reduced to a skeleton in which, nevertheless, the essential facts are still recognisable, until towards the end of the scherzo hardly more than the top part and the bass are left. Of the following trio only the first section is sketched, a scanty waltz tune. The composer could not bring himself to add even a bass line to it; and with the end of these sixteen bars the sketch peters out.

Even the external facts of this manuscript, as described, add up to an almost clinical picture of increasingly reluctant work, continued more out of a sense of duty than in response to a genuine urge. If one then actually reads this music, the impression is simply shattering. This is Schubert without the blessing of inspiration. This blunt unison four-bar phrase, whose continuation is merely a restatement a third lower, might just be acceptable as an opening if something more

[1] Since this was written, an additional page of the full score, which exactly follows the sketch, has been found.

imaginative were to follow immediately to set it in relief. But there is nothing of the kind; the phrase makes itself more comfortable by changing over to the major key, starts again from the beginning and arrives without any further ado at the first double bar. As can be seen in so many of Schubert's scherzos, the beginning of the following section would be the most suitable place for an enlargement of the vista by the introduction of a new idea. But this fails to materialise. The unfortunate first phrase goes on without reprieve. It clutches at its third bar which, restated over and over again, moves on in sequences. No end of this miserable little three-note motif! Those who go in for such subtleties may derive some satisfaction from the discovery that in these three notes the fourth bar of the first movement returns in inversion, and may hail a supposed "ur-motif". But this is no help either. It may easily be the only Schubert scherzo in which there is no hint at any further melodic invention beyond the initial phrase. And no trace of Schubert's usually so colourful harmonic exploits, with their wide tonal horizon and rich modulation; everything moves almost anxiously within a narrow orbit. The waltz tune sketched for the trio hardly rises above the most home-spun that one can find in Schubert's sets of dances. And after this waltz opening there was evidently nothing more he could do.

Quite apart from the quality, the mere size of a scherzo appropriate to a symphonic lay-out is an important factor. What a fully developed, abundant scherzo by Schubert looks like is shown by works such as the Great Symphony in C major, the Octet, or the String Quintet. He must have realised that such a narrow-chested construction, even if perhaps adequate for a modest sonata, could hardly do for a symphony, least of all after those two monumental movements.

The temporary failure of creative power, which can be observed here in such a drastic form, is nothing unusual in the artistic process, and the greatest were not immune to it. One might call it a periodic condition which can happen at any time to an artist. It is a depressing condition. Beethoven, Wagner and Verdi suffered from it for years, Wolf often complains of it in his letters. But the mature artist recognises the symptoms and knows they will pass. What triggers it off is almost invariably a piece of work that has reached an impasse. To come to terms with such problems requires self-confidence, resoluteness, a secure instinct strengthened by experience, and the patience to wait until the productive mind has become ready to do its work once more. The noble essence has to be distilled from a confused mass of raw material. The utmost clear-mindedness and an unshakeable determination is needed when what already seemed almost within grasp of the imagination becomes blurred, or threatens to disappear altogether. Such situations can be seen everywhere in Schubert's abandoned fragments, as has been described. The composer feels as though he has become lost in the scrub and cannot find his way through. There is nothing he can do but go back, like the Alpine climber, to the place where he went astray, and try to find the right path from there. Those interested in such things will find amazing illustrations of this in Beethoven's sketch-books, as edited by Nottebohm. Beethoven's procedure is fundamentally different from what usually happens in a sketch: subsequent retouching of minor deficiencies that have occured in a first draft. This latter procedure is frequently found with Schubert, as with others. For natural reasons, this is usually a matter of expanding the original invention, or deleting superfluous prolixity. Extensive reshaping of a sketch, however, occurs only in Schubert's last instrumental venture, the three piano sonatas of September 1828. Particularly in the finale of the great Sonata in A major there are remarkable things. Here he went back to the beginning of an already fully finished subsidiary episode, crossing out everything he had written and putting a new invention of incomparably larger design in its place, thus producing a new impulse and totally different dimensions. The mature method of working which can be recognised in this, in conjunction with the studies in counterpoint started at that time, almost give the impression that he had arrived at the threshold of a new creative period which he would not live to see.

These sonatas, however, date from six years after that unfortunate scherzo in B minor. What happened in the latter was a relapse into old inadequacies. As in so many other cases considered earlier, the root of the evil lay in an unsuccessful opening from which the composer was not able to break away.

As his friends relate, he was in the habit of spending every morning at his desk. It may have been an unlucky day; even Schubert could have days when the right inspiration refused to come. He may just have started his accustomed work over-tired and sleepy, without really feeling like it, quickly putting on paper this beginning of a scherzo, and writing down whatever followed immediately from it. We know of the speed with which he worked. He may have put down this sketch as fast as his pen could write. All this is of no consequence; the im-portant thing is that this unfortunate improvisation had forced its way in, and it will be remembered how difficult it was for Schubert to shake off such a *fait accompli*. It is clear that he had no pleasure in it; we are told this unequivocally by the increasing reluctance of the sketch. There is no more typical example of an artistic miscarriage. He interrupted his work after the first part of the trio, and left it at that for the time being.

What has been described here, and emerges fairly unambigu-ously from the sketch, could have happened to anybody. That it led to a tragic failure in this case was due to Schubert's character, his habits, and his lack of self-confidence; but perhaps also to his loneliness. He had no-one to whom he could show his work, no-one to give him support and advice. Reading the exchange of letters between young Brahms and Joachim, one realises how immensely beneficial the critical understanding of a knowledgeable friend can be for an artist. Schubert must have known at that time that he had reached for the stars. The assumption that he was not conscious of the significance of his work is an absurdity which can only be perpetrated by someone who has not the faintest inkling of what goes on in an artist's mind. The writer of these two move-ments must have experienced the creator's joy in all its ecstasy. This first half of a symphony, which makes its own inexorable demands, must have filled his heart with the consciousness, as crushing as it was elevating, of a profound obligation. And then came that precipitate, unsuccessful draft of a scherzo!

Others would have waited, would have laid it aside and taken it up again after some time with a free mind and a fresh hand. This Schubert was unable to do. To invent music was his form of addiction, something he could not do without;

this scherzo was a spectre that haunted him, blocking his invention. The only remedy was a new creative venture which would clear his head, and this was soon found, as we can gather from his own record. The radiant, open world of the "Wanderer" Fantasy presented itself. As always in such circumstances, he found an escape in a new work, and thus, for the time being, the crisis was overcome. But this was self-deception; an unfinished work is a heavy burden on the conscience.

In order to understand why Schubert failed on this occasion, it is essential to consider the principle of symphonic form. This structure of four movements, independently invented and worked out, yet complementing each other, was the result of a long development over generations. Through Beethoven it had received the stamp of organic necessity, and Schubert would never have dreamt of departing from this principle. Symphonic structure, in this sense, implies a hardly definable unity of character in spite of the individuality of each single movement. It will be easily recalled that every Beethoven symphony has its own unmistakable style and character. This should be all the more true of a composer whose work is primarily and so irresistibly determined by its emotional content as Schubert's. This unity in spite of all contrasting diversity is based upon an intuitive creative act, as is everything pertaining to the enigma of style. To hunt for "ur-motifs" in a symphony is a cheap expedient. It can happen that, as if involuntarily, certain turns of phrase carry over from one movement to another; but this is accidental. Had Beethoven ever contemplated such a thing, his sketch-books would tell us about it. When a composer has such an intention, he makes it abundantly clear, as Brahms, for example, did in his symphonies. But otherwise it is an idle pursuit to take three notes and prove their presence in every movement. The same sequence of notes may easily be found in any other of the composer's works. The genuine inner connections between the four movements of a symphony are—apart from key relationships—far, far more subtle, and just as hard to define as, for instance, the stylistic unity of a Mozart opera. Not only would it be difficult to imagine an aria from *Figaro* transplanted into *The Magic Flute*, but even the arias of Donna Anna, Zerlina or Elvira in *Don Giovanni* speak their own personal idioms and could hardly be transferred from one to the other. To explore the conditions governing such stylistic peculiarities, which are based on certain patterns of time, harmony, or phrasing, would be very much more arduous than chasing after illusory "ur-motifs".

It will easily be understood that it is here that one of the main problems of true symphonic style is to be found. The composer of "Ganymed", "Erlkönig" and "Der Wanderer" had no difficulty in shaping a movement charged with emotion and growing organically. This could be done in a single, concentrated creative act, springing directly from the first impulse. In a symphony, the problem consisted in maintaining such inspiration as a permanent state, as it were, as a live source of invention from which to create three further movements, differing in character and yet coming from the same emotional sphere. This presupposes a sureness and depth of conception such as Schubert was not able to achieve until the last five years of his life. He had previously foundered on this rock all too often, and this applies to the Symphony in B minor as well as, for example, the Quartet Movement in C minor. Moreover, it is clear that such emotionally charged conceptions posed far more difficult problems of this kind than the bright, sunny world of the "Trout" Quintet.

The lyricist is more dependent than any other on his daily state of mind. Only through further years of continuous effort did Schubert learn the difficult art of letting a great symphonic form grow and ripen to its full maturity. At the time of the Unfinished Symphony he had not yet found the inner discipline to have a comprehensive, overall view of every detail of a monumental form-complex. The two movements had succeeded in a way that must have seemed like a miracle to Schubert himself. In the flush of inspiration he was not conscious of the immense responsibility of the next step. He took this step, and had the misfortune to stumble. The sleepwalker's assurance had been lost. He could not get over this.

Everything that followed can be explained by the tormenting sense of his guilt over the unborn work and his incapacity to find a way back to the blessed world of his initial inspiration. This world had cut itself off from him; it was no longer accessible to his imagination. Other works had come in between, first the "Wanderer" Fantasy, then a dozen of his most glorious songs, finally, in the course of the following spring, *Die Verschworenen*, and during the summer and autumn *Fierabras*, *Die schöne Müllerin* and *Rosamunde*. And this was the year of his fateful illness! He did not have the will-power and energy which enabled Beethoven, Wagner, or Brahms, to return to a composition even after many years had passed, and to overcome problems which at first had seemed insoluble. At this stage of his development Schubert could only complete a work in a single burst, with the burning fire of the initial inspiration. Never in his life did he come back to a composition he had left unfinished, and one can only conclude that he must have had insuperable inhibitions in this respect.

So far we have been concerned with facts which can hardly be questioned. What follows is conjecture, based upon the image of Schubert that has emerged from all that has been said. There can be no doubt that the spectre in B minor, that skeleton in his cupboard, must have troubled him. No creative artist could have overcome such a failure with equanimity. He may occasionally have glanced at the manuscript, or even have tried to continue where he had left off. But then he would find that his mind was blank, his imagination paralysed. The thread was broken.

The discouragement of previous failures may have been a contributory factor. He was ailing and no doubt unspeakably miserable. When, in spring, he had promised a symphony to the Society in Graz, he may still have thought of this one and of the possibility of finishing it. Then, after the fateful summer, he did something desperate: he tore the work from his heart and gave the manuscript away, in order not to have it before his eyes any longer. It would never have crossed his mind that half a symphony could be performed. So it was immaterial to him who finally kept the manuscript. He never asked about it. He deliberately banished the work from his consciousness.

There are miracles which one fails to recognise as such as long as one has not thought about them. Here, a lonely man, hopelessly struggling, deliberately let his masterpiece disappear from sight because he despaired of completing it. As if by an act of self-preservation it rose from the dead after many, many years, and took its place where it belongs, among the greatest achievements of its kind.

Has anything more incredible ever happened?

And has anyone really given thought to yet another miracle: that from a disaster a work of art of the highest order has emerged? Whatever the reasons for its remaining unfinished, this cannot have been the intention of its creator. How, more than forty years later, even as experienced a conductor and as ardent a Schubertian as Herbeck could mistrust the effectiveness of such a symphonic fragment, can be seen from the circumstance mentioned: that he found it necessary to add to it a finale taken from one of Schubert's early symphonies. That this was redundant, even harmful, was presumably immediately evident. And now we have these two movements of almost equal length, with practically the same time-structure but in different keys, and yet the equilibrium and the harmonious juxtaposition in which they stand could not have been achieved more satisfactorily by the keenest artistic consciousness. This is a unique case, refuting all the principles of the century-old symphonic form. And it happened not as the result of an artist's vision, of a deliberate form-construction, but actually through the opposite, a failure, the collapse of what was originally intended as a traditional form!

Vienna prides itself in another monument that may give rise to similar aesthetic speculations: St Stephen's Cathedral. The fact that, contrary to the original plan, the traditional second spire was never built, for whatever reason, has contributed enormously to the unsurpassed magnificence of this building. It almost looks as if the true work of art had a secret existence of its own, an *élan vital* independent of the artist's will. As in all human matters, even in the purest realm of the spirit, in the genesis of a work of art, an element of chance remains active. Goethe may have experienced something of this sort with his own work. In a letter to Schiller he makes a curious remark that seems to point in this direction; it refers to the memoirs of Benvenuto Cellini, which he was busy translating at that time: "The casting of Perseus is indeed one of the highlights, showing that in the whole work on this statue, up to the very last moment, disposition of character, the artist's genius, craftsmanship, passion and chance all worked together, so that the work of art emerges as though it were a product of nature."

The "Unfinished" Symphony was the final crisis of Schubert's apprenticeship. The instrumental composer rose to the summit of his creative power. But he was still not secure from certain accidents to which an idea is exposed as long as it has not yet found its final mould. Between the large piano sonatas in A minor, Op. 42, and D major, Op. 53, from the year 1825, stands the fragment of a sonata in C major of equally large conception. The inspired and widely-spaced first movement and the beautiful, strongly-profiled *andante* are complete. After this the quality of the invention becomes questionable. An amiable minuet begins non-committally and soon becomes entangled in tonal by-ways from which it cannot find a way out, and the composer breaks off in the middle of a sentence, as it were, although he follows it up with a trio, which, however, does not get properly off the ground either. The finale starts in the manner of a *perpetuum mobile*, but does not really seem to enjoy its bustling, and a middle section, beginning after a lengthy exposition, runs, like the minuet, into the void, without even reaching the next comma.

It was Schubert's last mishap of this kind. But he had to wait until he was twenty-eight to learn Beethoven's patience.

However, there were also external reasons that could cause him to give up a work he had begun. One must not forget how limited his practical possibilities were, and how he always had to consider what use could be made of a composition on which he had embarked. He was easily filled with enthusiasm, but just as easily discouraged. Among the works which, after Schubert's death, his brother Ferdinand offered for sale to the Viennese publisher Diabelli, was an unfinished oratorio in three acts, *Lazarus*, extant in full score up to about the middle of the second act. The music, written in 1820, just before *Die Zauberharfe*, is the most original, most attractive example of Schubert's serious dramatic style. This pietistically sentimental sequence of scenes from the New Testament is treated throughout in an operatic manner. It conveys an impression of the way in which Schubert could have set about writing a through-composed opera, without the customary division into recitativo, arias and ensembles, following only the lyrical expression and the form structure arising from it—an anticipation of a method of operatic composition which was not to develop until one generation later. He may have given up working at it when there was no prospect of a performance, or he may have interrupted it in order to write the music for *Die Zauberharfe*, whose performance was imminent, and then not have found his way back. *Lazarus*, a highly significant work, is altogether shrouded in mystery. It has not even been possible to ascertain whether the existing fragment is all Schubert wrote, or if more was written but has been lost.

The first performance, apart from an attempt by Ferdinand shortly after Schubert's death, took place in Vienna in 1863 under Herbeck. Brahms writes about this to Joachim (3 April 1863): "You may have read that here a *Lazarus* by Schubert has celebrated his resurrection after forty-three years! I have copied out several scenes, and if you have the necessary time, and will be staying in Hanover for a while longer, I could send them to you, and promise you the greatest enjoyment."

But, like *Lazarus*, Schubert's numerous operas are to the reader "a sight both lovely and sad". That so many of them— *Der Spiegelritter, Sakuntala, Die Bürgschaft, Adrast, Der Graf von Gleichen*—remain unfinished, is symptomatic of the operatic composer's hopeless situation. The loveliness lies in the immense wealth of beautiful, original music that he has lavished on his operas. The sadness is in their incorrigible dramatic ineptitude. Wherever one opens such a score as *Alfonso und Estrella* or *Fierabras*, a gem of Schubertian invention leaps out, a melody such as only he could invent, an ecstatic, blissful moment of rapture. But if one reads the words of such a scene, one becomes depressed and cannot imagine how anything of this sort could possibly be put on the stage. Occasional attempts at productions of *Fierabras, Alfonso und Estrella* or *Der vierjährige Posten* have not been encouraging. Only the unassuming one-act singspiel *Die Verschworenen* has so far managed to keep Schubert's dramatic music at least sporadically alive. This is a meagre outcome after endless efforts. The glory which Schubert could have created for German opera never materialised.

8

CHARACTER AND DESTINY

"In deiner Brust sind deines Schicksals Sterne."
                                    SCHILLER
("In thy breast are thy destiny's stars.")

IN CONTEMPLATING THE events of Schubert's life and his position in the world, one cannot help feeling that everything that happened to him arose from the peculiarity of his nature, indeed that he was subject to a destiny which inevitably determined his fate. It lay in his character, in the defencelessness of a man without the drive to assert himself. "I will seize destiny by the throat!" This sounds melodramatic enough to be a fabrication, but it actually occurs in one of Beethoven's letters, and the same is true of the utterance: "Force is the morality of those who are superior to others, and it is mine too." Thoughts like these would never have entered Schubert's head. But Beethoven was a contemporary of Napoleon, and wrote a Heroic Symphony. Schubert belonged to an unheroic generation. His career would have been different had he possessed but a spark of Beethoven's will-power. He never approached the banquet of life except with a shy request to be admitted. Anyone who does this will be badly treated.

This lack of drive and his passive response to any external pressure were certainly rooted in his constitution. The glory of his music stems from a world of fantasy which lies beyond any narrow dictates of the will. Even when Beethoven starts in an altogether relaxed and amiable mood, as in his Violin Concerto, the tenth bar already sounds an imperious note, shaking the listener out of his comfortable repose. And even when Schubert's conception is centred in a tragic conflict, with a dynamic impetus, as in the first movement of his String Quartet in D minor ("Death and the Maiden"), over and over again it is lyrical expressiveness, even idyllic relaxation, which gains the upper hand. Death stands in the background as a dark menace, but the centre of the picture, the focus of his feelings, is the maiden. The introverted, contemplative nature which deprived Schubert of any power of resistance in life bestowed on his music its immeasurable wealth. He himself understood only too well how ill-equipped he was for the struggle for existence, when he wrote to his friend Bauernfeld: "I can already see you as *Hofrat* [high-ranking civil servant] and successful playwright. But what about me! What will become of a poor musician like me? In my old age I shall probably have to slink from door to door like Goethe's Harpist, begging for bread. . . ."

Books are known to have their fates, and the same can sometimes be said of tunes. One of Schubert's has undergone adventures which are symptomatic of his situation, and, more generally, of the lack of legal protection for intellectual property at that time. In 1821 Schubert's first waltzes, Op. 9, were published, a set of thirty-six short dance tunes, written several years earlier. One of these pieces, No. 2, had become a special favourite with Schubert's friends, under the curious title "Trauerwalzer" ("Sorrow Waltz"). The inevitable Anselm Hüttenbrenner owned a handwritten copy of it, to which Schubert had added a jocular dedication: "Written for my coffee, wine and punch companion Anselm Hüttenbrenner, world-famous composer. Vienna, 14 March in the year of our Lord 1818, in his very own most exalted abode, at 30 florins." His authorship is thus not in doubt; but it is also unmistakably imprinted on the tune itself, which was always one of his most popular, and, fitted out with atrocious words, finally toured the world as a hit in "Lilac Time".

Here it is:

What makes the tune so attractive and catchy is the expressive curve of the first phrase; but its real, decisive quality lies in the second phrase, with the imaginative breadth of its harmonic perspective. The first eight bars could just possibly have been invented by someone else. No doubt could ever have been raised, however, about the second section, with its wonderful, most characteristic Schubertian rapture. All the same, this tune was simply pilfered from him and gained incredible popularity in numerous not only German but also English and French editions. At first it was treated anonymously. There appeared *Variations on the popular Sorrow Waltz* by Johann Pensel, an obscure contemporary of Schubert's, and, soon afterwards, *Variations on a favourite Viennese Waltz* by Carl Czerny. A few years later, for the sake of simplicity, the tune was ascribed to Beethoven—even by his own publisher, Schott, who obviously expected better sales from the famous name. From then on, in spite of his explicit denial, it was Beethoven who, as far as the world was concerned, remained the inventor of this tune, which was now named *Sehnsuchtswalzer* (Waltz of Longing). There is no record of any comment from Schubert on this expropriation. Why should he bother about some old tune or other? He could write a new one any day. Only in the complete edition of his works, more than half a century later, was this error unequivocally rectified.

Schubert's fate is so deeply disturbing because it demonstrates so forcefully how the world, with callous unconcern, will treat as a troublesome beggar anyone who cannot summon up the necessary self-assurance to demand rather than request. It is possible that his lowly origins, his needy circumstances and his small stature contributed to his shyness. There is no doubt, however, that all the humiliations he had experienced in his youth, from the enforced choice of profession to all the unsuccessful applications, must have played a part in the lack of self-confidence which inhibited him in all his enterprises. It is said that nothing succeeds like success. Conversely, nothing is more demoralising than continuous failure. Yet one must certainly not assume that his music was not appreciated. There would have been no Schubertians and no Schubertiads had his friends not experienced the keenest pleasure in what he had to offer. But this was a closed circle beyond which his music all too rarely penetrated. The amazing thing is that, from all appearances, it does not seem to have occurred to any of these friends that it was immortal music to which they had been listening when Vogl, accompanied by Schubert, sang "Erlkönig", "Der Wanderer", "Ganymed" or "Grenzen der Menschheit". They were pleased to have such a talented friend, and found it nice that he was so modest and unassuming and left all the honour of the occasion to the worthy singer. One might do even more for him and buy a few books of his songs. And in the end, when he had become famous, one wrote reminiscences of him and ascertained from the distance of a few decades that he had been a highly gifted young man and might even have achieved a good deal more, had he had a longer life.

Did no one sense how a whole generation of contemporaries had sinned against one of the elect? The behaviour of posterity almost gives one to believe that such a feeling of collective guilt did exist in Vienna, and that people tried to rid themselves of it by trivialising the case. It is only natural to appease one's guilty conscience by continuing not to take too seriously the victim of one's misjudgment. The fate and adventures of Schubert's artistic legacy tell us a great deal about this, and some details of interest may be added here.

Immediately after his death there were some obituaries and a memorial concert in Vienna. His brother Ferdinand did his utmost for the music Schubert had left. At that time the public at large had as yet hardly taken notice of him. Then his songs began to circulate more widely. But when, six years later, one of the most prominent musical notables in Vienna, the music historian Raphael Georg Kiesewetter, who belonged to the circle of Schubert's friends, published a *History of European-Occidental Music*, he called the most recent period, extending from 1800 to 1832, "The Epoch of Beethoven and Rossini", and found it unnecessary even to mention Schubert's name. In view of this, there would be no reason to expect foreign publications to be better informed. Sainsbury's *Dictionary of Music*, published in London in 1827, does contain the name Franz Schubert; but the entry refers only to a namesake, a Dresden violinist.

Nevertheless, the Viennese publisher Diabelli did at that time go to great expense to acquire the bulk of Schubert's unpublished music, as far as it was of interest to him, for the sum of 2,400 florins (about £240). This comprised fifty books of songs and dozens of other works of all kinds, though excluding the symphonies and operas. But he delayed over printing them. Three of the greatest chamber music works, the Octet, the String Quintet, and the String Quartet in G major, remained in his vaults for twenty years before they even saw their first performance, and other works were kept under lock and key by Diabelli's successor Spina until the seventies. When Brahms moved to Vienna in 1862, he tried to interest his publisher Rieter-Biedermann of Winterthur in Schubert's unpublished music. "My best hours here", he wrote, "I owe to unprinted works by Schubert, of which I have quite a number at home in manuscript. Yet, however delightful and enjoyable it is to contemplate them, everything else about this music is sad. I have, for instance, many things here in manuscript, belonging to Spina or Schneider [nephew of Schubert], of which nothing exists but just the manuscript, not a single copy! And neither at Spina's nor with me are they kept in fireproof cabinets. A whole pile of unprinted music was recently offered for sale at an incredibly low price, and, fortunately, the Society of Friends of Music were still able to buy it. How many things there are scattered here and there among private individuals who either guard their treasures like dragons or carelessly let them disappear!" He could not have had an inkling how precisely both statements applied to Schubert's friend Anselm Hüttenbrenner.

It was only with considerable hesitation that the Swiss publisher took the opportunity. Like his colleagues in Vienna he evidently mistrusted this stuff which had already been lying around for so long. All the same, he did at that time publish the great Mass in E flat, to which Brahms anonymously contributed a vocal score, and also some piano compositions. But the first six symphonies, together with numerous other works, comprising all the operas and hundreds of songs, had to wait until the publication of the Complete Edition.

The strange thing is that Schubert's instrumental music was consistently ignored for so long, and that even his first biographer, Kreissle, who revived interest in him in the sixties, showed considerably less conviction when standing up for his instrumental works than with regard to the songs, which, to be sure, had won general appreciation soon after Schubert's death, even outside the German-speaking countries.

The discovery of the great Symphony in C major was, of course, a turning point of the deepest significance. Schubert's symphonic music had been buried alive in his manuscripts until, in 1839, Schumann rescued it from oblivion through his memorable initiative. It is characteristic of the situation in Vienna that people seemed reluctant to take cognisance of this fact. It was, after all, rather annoying that a fellow should have come from Germany to stick his nose into Viennese affairs and make a "discovery" which was not new to anyone. Ferdinand had done his best with his brother's symphonies but had not succeeded in arousing any interest in them. All the same, half a year later a performance of the work that had been such a sensation in Leipzig and about which long articles had appeared in foreign papers could not really be avoided in Vienna. But at the last moment there were misgivings; two movements had to suffice, with an aria from Donizetti's *Lucia di Lammermoor* inserted between them, as if to ask the audience's forgiveness for such an imposition. The Viennese had to wait another eleven years before they were offered a complete performance of this symphony. It was too difficult, too extensive, and therefore too inconvenient, and it was still to take a long time to find a place in the repertoire.

It may at first have been the unusual breadth of design which appeared strange to a public that did not expect any-

thing of this nature in a concert and, apart from the well-
established symphonies of Beethoven, found those by Spohr
or Mendelssohn much easier to digest. But it must nevertheless
have been the consequence of some deep-seated prejudice that,
for another half century, the most extraordinary quality of
Schubert's world, its greatness, its sublimity, its majesty of
stature, were simply not appreciated at all. A homely, idyllic
world, heightened to monumentality! This did not tally with
the image one had formed of this composer. From the first
pronouncements by his devoted friends, from the striking
success of easily-remembered tunes, the public had so misunderstood his nature as to make this misconception well-nigh
ineradicable. Everything contributed to confirm this fiction.
It has been mentioned how much it may be blamed on personal
reminiscences of dubious reliability. It proved impossible to
remove their philistine connotations from his person, and the
circumstance that the environment in which he lived and
created was undoubtedly easy-going and comfortably middle-
class, made it difficult for his true character as a man and an
artist to be recognised. That he never expressed himself in words
—and nothing is more characteristic of him than just this—makes
it understandable that none of his friends were able to perceive
more than his outer shell. This unpretentious cover betrayed
nothing of the gigantic visions that dwelt in his imagination
and took shape in his work. Beethoven, the Titan, kept his
friends at arm's length. Schubert shared the cosy conviviality
of his fellows and had to pay the penalty for it. If it is justifiable
to identify the artist with the man, a false image of the latter
becomes all the more dangerous.

Schubert would not have been made an operetta-hero if
people had had the faintest notion of the tragedy that was his
life. A life continually overshadowed; a life of permanent
material need and dependence; a life of repeated rejection.
Can one comprehend what to be consistently ignored means
to a man who is fully conscious of his achievement and his
unlimited capability? And a life without the blessing of love!
This may well have been the bitterest and most tragic circumstance, which explains much and was the cause of much. As
already mentioned, there is no evidence that Schubert had any
love-relationships to which any significance could be attached.

An artist of the highest sensibility, a man whose deep natural sensuousness is unmistakable in the rich sound of his music, must have been as subject to Eros as anyone else. He was small, tending to corpulence, inhibited by shyness, and probably found it as difficult to woo as to win respect. That he himself had experienced the sufferings of his young miller, the misery of his winter traveller, with the hundredfold intensity of a highly sensitive human being with a burning imagination— his songs bear witness to all this. His friends were fast-living men of the world. The society in which he lived was anything but puritanical in attitude. It is a symbol of his condition that he sat at the piano playing while the others were dancing. It looks like an inevitable consequence that Venus had nothing left for him but the scraps from her rich table. What she had to give him were disappointments, sufferings and an insidious, destructive illness. One cannot imagine what this misfortune must have meant for a keenly sensitive person. Even purely psychologically he could never have overcome it.

Did anyone know of this tragic background to his life? The only one to allude to it was Schober. At Schubert's funeral service a poem of his was sung in Church to the tune of Schubert's song "Pax vobiscum". It contains the following lines:

> For many roses did this life on earth
> With pointed thorns reward thee for thy worth,
> With pain and sorrow and an early grave.

As one knows, a tragic life has all too often been the price a genius has had to pay for being one of the elect. What really matters is the fulfilment he has achieved in his work. But even here, behind the facts, loom tragic aspects which have rarely been grasped to their full extent. The sign of the *Unfinished*, which has been embodied in one of his greatest creations, stands above Schubert's life and achievements like an inescapably predetermined fate. His work, which impresses us with such greatness and magnificence, has likewise remained unfinished. To assess in some measure the significance of his early death, we must examine the relationship between achievement and duration of life in other artists of the highest rank.

Though inestimable treasures have been lost with all those who were not granted their full span of life, each of the great composers, with the sole exception of Schubert, could leave behind him a fully-rounded life's work. Yet none of them attained his greatest and most significant peak before the fourth decade of his life. Even Mozart, the most precocious, was, at the age of thirty, only at the threshold of the period that was to see the summit of his achievement. Had he died at Schubert's age there would have been no *Così fan tutte*, no *Magic Flute*, no *Requiem*, and none of the late symphonies, string quintets or piano concertos. Handel before his oratorios, Bach before Cöthen and Leipzig, Haydn at the beginning of his proper career, Beethoven before his Second Symphony, Wagner before *Lohengrin*: what would we know of them? It is not even possible to pass judgment on the latent potentialities of the operatic composer. Had Weber died at Schubert's age, neither *Freischütz* nor *Euryanthe* nor *Oberon* would have seen the light of day.

Schubert left a full life's work in his songs, thanks to his early mastery in this field. His *lieder* form a totality, integrated and complete. Whatever precious additions might still have accrued, these would not, as far as one can judge, essentially have altered the impression. It is different with the instrumental composer, who had reached his full maturity comparatively late. His laborious progress, with its many afflictions, has been described, with the Symphony in B minor as the tragic monument to his struggles. Only during the last five years of his life does he seem to have attained the fullest mastery, the noblest greatness of vision and aim. From the amount of great creations he was nevertheless able to leave behind him, and from the desperately short time he was granted to produce them, one may to some extent surmise what has been irretrievably buried with him. This is Atlantis, a sunken world!

Seen from this point of view, Grillparzer's epitaph, "Great riches but still richer hopes", was apt. However, Grillparzer lacked any notion of the gigantic stature of the phenomenon with which he was dealing. On the other hand, who would have guessed that of the unpretentious little man?

One must not be unjust. Contemporaries rarely see more than the tip of the iceberg. What Schubert's can be accused of is that they did not *want* to see more, even when his songs had become more and more widely known, and at least such eminent experts as Schumann began to realise his true significance.

At that time the trouble was that Schubert's most important works were unknown because they were inaccessible. Strangely enough, the danger today is that Schubert can be underrated for the opposite reason, namely because juvenilia are placed far too indiscriminately and uncritically next to mature and outstanding works, tending to blur the image of one of the greatest of the great. The principal deficiency of his early instrumental music is not so much the immaturity of its style as the insubstantial nature of its thematic material, which moves with youthful unconcern in well-established grooves. Even in his Fifth Symphony there is still a minuet so audibly derived from Mozart's G minor Symphony that one cannot help comparing—and noticing how enormously the original surpasses the stylistic copy. No major composer started any differently, and the phenomenon is perfectly normal and natural for the state of Schubert's development as an instrumental composer at that time. What always delights, and makes even his juvenilia so lovable, is their freshness and grace, and this, as for example in the *andante* movements of his Fifth and Sixth Symphonies, is always irresistible. But the serene world of such movements in which the born lyricist reveals himself is not matched by anything in the outer movements which could in the true sense be called symphonic. The mature Schubert did achieve this most magnificently, not by the nuclear force of dynamically interacting motifs, like Beethoven or Brahms, but by a monumental vision of the eternal, which is a feature of the true, great Schubert, as it is of Bruckner, who has a curious, elusive affinity with him, a common background that can probably only be understood in terms of an emotional landscape. The young song-writer had already found his way to such heights of monumentality at an early stage when the poetic word stirred his receptive imagination, and none of his successors in this sphere of the *lied* ever approached him—except perhaps, on one single occasion and in a quite different manner, Brahms, in his *Four Serious Songs*. The dew-fresh charm of Schubert's Fifth Symphony is to his great symphonic works what, say,

"Heidenröslein" is to "An Schwager Kronos", with the difference that the perfection of a miniature is possible in a song but not in a symphony or a string quartet.

One must be clear about such elementary facts where absolute values are concerned. It was indeed worthwhile to have brought to light those six early symphonies, twelve early string quartets and so many rondos, overtures and variations. But today, when there is an insatiable demand for music and relative lack of discrimination on the part of a record-buying public, and when the commercial value of a famous name may be the sole criterion for the industry profiting from it, it is hardly avoidable that a master's image should become tarnished when music is constantly being heard under his name which should be appreciated only in relative terms. As has been explained here, Schubert's case is fundamentally different from that of all the others whose music we love and venerate. Beside his representative works his juvenilia appear like foothills beside Alpine peaks. Those who love him will also enjoy spending some time on these foothills, but they should realise that the fame of the instrumental composer rests on not much more than a dozen or so items of orchestral and chamber music and a dozen piano works, equal to the greatest of their kind. The number is not impressive; but it is the weight that counts. And as far as the volume of what he has created is concerned, the greatness of his songs, in bulk as well as in intrinsic value, has remained unrivalled, quite apart from the splendours of his choral music, his sacred music, his precious piano duets, and the sunken treasure of his operas. The amount of music that sprang from this short life, beset with every imaginable external adversity, remains unbelievable.

The world that a human mind erects for itself is something unique and wholly individual. Nature has never repeated itself in the creation of genius. This is why it is so necessary to come as close as possible to a great artist's character if one wishes to acquire a deeper understanding of his work. Since with Schubert everything flows from spontaneous feeling, his music is a mirror of his soul. With none of the other great masters is the bridge from the world of feeling to its expression in the work of art so direct; the reason is that with Schubert conscious reflection plays such a subordinate part in the creative act.

And no other composer has expressed himself to such an extent with music's most immediate means of communication, melody. The listener is never in danger of misunderstanding it as long as it comes to him pure and unadulterated.

Here, however, lies the basic problem of all music: it is dependent on its execution. A person of acute perception recognises instantly the difference between an inspired performance, reflecting the true spirit of the work of art, and an indifferent rendering. But even the most naïve listener will instinctively notice this difference when Schubert's most natural form of expression, the *lied*, is concerned, although he may not be conscious of the reasons. The breathing, the colour of a vowel, the minutest accent, the subtle articulation of a consonant can be decisive for the meaningful shaping of a phrase. All this is familiar to the well-trained, artistically responsible singer. But all too often even gifted and accomplished instrumentalists do not realise to what an enormous extent the effect of Schubert's music depends on a manner of phrasing and articulation that stems from a vocal conception. Anyone who approaches a Schubert symphony by way of time-beating, bowing, or dynamic contrast, has missed its true character, and the same can be said of a pianist who, in the wood of brilliant passage work, does not perceive the trees of continuous melody from which a Schubert sonata movement or impromptu has grown. For his instrumental style as for his songs the negative rule applies, that his music must never become subservient to the metronome. The melody soars freely and wonderfully. It is not subject to gravity, however much it has, like any musical utterance, to obey the fundamental condition for all freedom, the discipline of form.

Just as Schubert's melody, when it reached maturity, was shaped by the words, a poetic element always remained the source of its expressiveness. This is the secret of its emotional impact. Schubert's greatness lies in the depth of this emotional experience. However miserable his existence must often have been during those last, dangerously threatened years, his optimism breaks through over and over again, his pleasure in the physical experience of life, in the beauty of a world which is full of riches for anyone able to look at it with fresh eyes every day, the beauty of a world of spring and youth:

Die Welt wird schöner mit jedem Tag,
Man weiss nicht, was noch werden mag,
Das Blühen will nicht enden...

(The world's more beauteous every day,
We know not what may come our way,
The flowering never ceases....)

Schubert sang one of his most blissful melodies to these lines by Uhland. His faith in spring was unshakeable. He lived for the joy and fervour of the act of creation. But every human personality has various sides; there is no doubt that his also contained a Phaeacian streak. He is the only one of the great who could idealise the everyday world. Anyone who is too unimaginative to be grateful for and enjoy this aspect of Schubert's idiom, this delight in the gift of life and its expression in the homeliest colloquial terms, lacks an essential organ of perception. Fate, which thrust this precious vessel of grace defenceless into the world, gave him the capacity to rejoice, and this it was that made him rich. From this wealth he drew the love that lives in his melodies, the love he never received and always so lavishly poured forth.

Since then the world has not stood still. The sounding brass and the tinkling cymbal have made amazing progress.

But what has happened to love?

APPENDICES

CHRONOLOGY

1785   Schubert's parents, Franz Theodor Schubert of Neudorf, Moravia, and Elisabeth Vietz of Zuckmantel, Silesia, married 7 January, Lichtenthal Parish Church, Vienna.

1797   Franz Peter Schubert born 31 January, 42 Himmelpfortgrund, Lichtenthal.

1808   Franz Schubert enters the Court Chapel in Vienna and the school attached to it.

1810   His first surviving composition, a Fantasy for piano duet, written 8 April–1 May.

1811   His first song, "Hagars Klage", written 30 March.

1812   Death of his mother, 28 May. Schubert's first larger compositions (sacred music, overtures).

1814   Schubert starts his activity as an assistant teacher at his father's school in Lichtenthal. First Mass (F major); first masterpieces of the *lied*; first opera, *Des Teufels Lustschloss*.

1815   More than 150 *lieder*, among them "Erlkönig" and "Rastlose Liebe".

1816   Unsuccessful application for a job at Ljubliana. Schubert leaves the school and moves to Schober.

1818   First public performance of a composition by Schubert, Italian Overture in C major (1 March). First summer vacation at Zseliz in Hungary.

1819   "Trout" Quintet; the lost cantata *Prometheus*.

1820   The oratorio *Lazarus*. Performance of Schubert's opera *Die Zwillingsbrüder* at the Kärntnertortheater in Vienna (14 July). Performance of *Die Zauberharfe* at the Theater an der Wien (19 August).

1821   Sketch of a symphony in E major–E minor.

1822   Opera *Alfonso und Estrella*; Symphony in B minor ("The Unfinished"); "Wanderer" Fantasy.

1823   Operas *Die Verschworenen* and *Fierabras*. Performance of *Rosamunde* (20 December). *Die schöne Müllerin*. Grave illness (summer and autumn).

1824   Second summer vacation at Zseliz. Octet; String Quartets in A minor and D minor; *Divertissement à l'Hongroise*.

1825   Holiday trip with Michael Vogl to Gmunden, Salzburg, Gastein. Piano Sonata in D major; Divertimento in E minor for piano duet.

1826   Unsuccessful application for position of Deputy Director of the Court Chapel. String Quartet in G major.

1827   *Winterreise*; Piano Trios in B flat major and E flat major. Beethoven's funeral (28 March), in which Schubert took part as a torch-bearer.

1828   His first and only public recital, given in Vienna 26 March. Great Symphony in C major; Mass in E flat; String Quintet; last fourteen songs, published after his death as *Schwanengesang* (Swan Song); last three piano sonatas, published as Op. posth. Ill with typhoid (beginning of November); death on 19 November.

SELECTED BIBLIOGRAPHY

Complete Edition of Schubert's Works, Editors' Report (E. Mandy-czewski, J. N. Fuchs, J. Brüll, J. Epstein)

O. E. Deutsch, *Schubert, Documents of his Life and Work* (London, 1946)

O. E. Deutsch, *Thematic Catalogue of Schubert's Works* (London, 1948)

Franz Schubert, Briefe und Schriften, ed. by O. E. Deutsch (Munich, 1919)

Schubert, die Erinnerungen seiner Freunde, ed. O. E. Deutsch (Leipzig, 1957)

M. G. E. Brown, *Franz Schubert, a Critical Biography* (London, 1958)

M. G. E. Brown, *Essays on Schubert* (London, 1966)

Richard Capell, *Schubert's Songs* (London, 1928)

Wilhelm von Chézy, *Erinnerungen aus meinem Leben* (Vienna, 1863)

Alfred Einstein, *Schubert* (New York, 1951)

Thrasybulos Georgiades, *Schubert, Musik und Lyrik* (Göttingen, 1967)

INDEX OF WORKS BY SCHUBERT MENTIONED
IN THE TEXT

INDEX OF PERSONS MENTIONED AND WORKS BY OTHER COMPOSERS